Motown, Stax and the Black Fight for Freedom 1960-1972

Annabel May Polles

(BAHons, MA)

Published in 2023 by FeedARead Publishing
Copyright © Annabel May Polles 2021
Copyright Cover/Illustration © Samantha Munro 2023

The author(s) assert the moral right under the Copyright, Designs and Patents Act 1988 to be identified as the author(s) of this work.

All Rights reserved. No part of this publication may be reproduced, stored in a retrieval system, or transmitted, in any form or by any means without the prior written consent of the publisher, nor be otherwise circulated in any form of binding or cover other than that in which it is published and without a similar condition being imposed on the subsequent purchaser.

British Library C.I.P.

A CIP catalogue record for this title is available from the British Library.

In honour of the music that made me who I am today

Acknowledgements

When I had the initial inspiration for this dissertation, I had great knowledge of the music but little knowledge on how it affected the black freedom struggle of the sixties and seventies. Fortunately, my passion for the music evolved into determination and I have stumbled across some of the most inspiring and knowledge-enhancing works I have ever discovered whilst being in higher education. I have many to thank for their support, encouragement, knowledge, insight, and time that allowed me to strive at researching this topic and producing a writing that not only adds to the field but also does it justice.

Firstly, and by no means are these acknowledgements in order of importance, I must thank the library staff at Keele University for purchasing all my order requests and thus providing this thesis with the background knowledge of the most important scholars in the field. I would have not been able to submit my thesis at a substantial standard without the books and autobiographies that they willingly purchased me.

Secondly, I would also like to thank my supervisor Dr David Ballantyne for providing an excellent module surrounding the civil rights movement from the second world war up until the mid-seventies. The module provided me with great context and introduced me to the wide literature and knowledge of the many historians that have been influential to my viewpoint and understanding of many layers of the civil rights movement and black freedom struggle. He also provided me with his expertise and recommended many books and articles, of topics I questioned him about, to supplement this dissertation. I would also like to thank him for his general support in every aspect, including all the Teams meetings we had.

Thirdly, I must thank David Ellis of the Motown Museum for being so willing to help this research and opening Motown's archives to my project. His support in the early days of this project kept me motivated to complete this writing when brick walls were hit. His unique insight and knowledge have had great influence on this thesis, and he has helped my love for Motown to grow even deeper.

Additionally, Craig Werner, the author of *A Change is Gonna Come: Music, Race and the Soul of America*, who I related to on many levels, deserves great acknowledgment and thanks for replying to my emails with such enthusiasm and giving me his own personal words of encouragement. Providing me with unique unpublished work he created in conjunction with Spike Lee and the contact details of other scholars, he also helped me to stay motivated and remember why I have such a passion for this topic.

I must also thank Charles Hughes, author of *Country Soul: Making Music and Making Race in the American South*, for showing such enthusiasm and interest in my project and providing me with much inside knowledge that has extremely influenced the writing of this dissertation. Organising a Zoom call, I managed to speak with Charles in Memphis who gave me so much to work with that accelerated my project forward. From primary sources such as the *Cash Box* magazine to secondary reading recommendations, his enthusiasm in his emails, and friendliness on Zoom, have kept me on track to complete this writing to the best I can in such little words.

Furthermore, I would also like to thank Brian Ward, author of *Just My Soul Responding: Rhythm and Blues, Black Consciousness and Race Relations* for replying to my emails and showing his expertise in those emails; where he offered his opinion on my topic and recommended readings to enhance my knowledge further.

Finally, I would like to thank Susanne Smith author of *Dancing in the Street* for responding to my email and encouraging me to carry on with this dissertation. Her book is an excellent write up surrounding Motown and Detroit in the mid-twentieth century.

Contents

Acknowledgements 5

Introduction: The Soul of America 15

'Ain't no place like Motown, Hitsville U.S.A': Community, Political Expression, Black Capitalism, and 'The Sound of Young America' 37

    Motown and the Black Community's 'Great March to Freedom' 45

    Money (That's What I Want) – Black Capitalism and Community Empowerment 63

    'What's Going On?' – Political Recordings and Political Expression 73

    'The Sound of Young America' – The Erosion of Racial Barriers 81

'634-5789 Soulsville, USA': Integration, Opportunity and Stax Fax 89

    Growing Green Onions and Planting the Seeds of Opportunity 99

    Stax Fax: 'Keeping Stax On the Coffee Table, When It Wasn't On the Turntable' 111

Conclusion: Black is Beautiful 141

About the Author 155

Bibliography 157

Figures

Figure 1 - Motown Record Company Logo 21
Figure 2 - Stax Record Company Logo 21
Figure 3 - View of men working on Ford cars assembly line 38
Figure 4 - Berry Gordy outside Motown Recording Studios 'Hitsville USA' 40
Figure 5 - Motown Stars Raise $25,000 For Poor Campaign. Jet Magazine, 23/5/1968 47
Figure 6 - Motown's Great March To Freedom Album 49
Figure 7 - Motown's 'The Great March to Freedom' album 49
Figure 8 - Martin Luther King Jr leading the march 52
Figure 9 - Detroit Free Press, 125,000 Walk Quietly in Record Rights Plea (24/6/1963) 53
Figure 10 - Thousands march down Woodward Avenue 54
Figure 11 - Front cover of The Illustrated News pamphlet on the Great March to Freedom 55
Figure 12 - Page 5 of the Illustrated News June 1963 edition 59
Figure 13 - Official Programme for the 'Great March to Freedom' 60
Figure 14 - Berry Gordy with numerous Motown albums 66
Figure 15 - Berry Gordy receiving an award from Small Business Week 71
Figure 16 - Writers of the Revolution album cover 74
Figure 17 - Free Huey album cover 74
Figure 18 - The Motown Sound Flyer 81
Figure 19 - Estelle Axton outside Stax 91
Figure 20 - Green Onions single record sleeve 100
Figure 21 - Cover page of Ebony article 101
Figure 22 - Booker T & the MG's 102
Figure 23 - Integrated Work Force Inside Stax Studio 104
Figure 24 - The Arizona Republic, Stax Records Define the Memphis Sound (24/6/1969) 105
Figure 25 - Billboard mentions Stay in School LP 111
Figure 26 – Pages 1 & 2 of Let's Save the Children 'The Staple Singers' ... 112
Figure 27 - Let's Save the Children 'The Staple Singers' 112
Figure 28 - Title of Stax Fax (Issue 7) 118
Figure 29 - 'Attention All Radio Announcers' Stax Fax Issue 9 (1969) 122
Figure 30 - Stax Fax for the 'Know' generation (Issue 10) 123
Figure 31 - 'Stay in School' (Issue 10) 125
Figure 32 - Stax Fax Cover with a picture of Dr King 133

Figure 33 - Comparative Calendar Issue 6 137
Figure 34 - Thank you message to Stax Fax editor Deanie Parker 139

Introduction: The Soul of America

African American music styles can be described as the sounds of both individual and collective 'identity realised' and 'proudly asserted' throughout the whole of America. They were sounds that accompanied the civil rights movement, reflecting the social changes and accomplishments of its own people. They were sounds that were the voice, and are the echo, of a time no one would 'want to see repeated'; these sounds were the 'poetry of the black revolution.'[1] As radio station owner and spokesmen, Shelley Stewart explained 'music really started breaking the barriers long before the politics in America began to deal with it. [The races] began to communicate… because of the music.'[2] As a member of the group The Platters also recalled, 'because of our music, white kids ventured into black areas. They had a sense of fair play long before the civil rights movement.'[3] With these testimonies, it is clear there is no question to why King proclaimed music as the 'soul of the [civil rights] movement.'[4] This writing, therefore, will argue that Soul and Rhythm and Blues music,

---

[1] P. Guralnick, *Sweet Soul Music: Rhythm and Blues and the Southern Dream of Freedom* (Edinburgh, 2002), p. 3; B. Ward, *Just My Soul Responding: Rhythm and Blues, Black Consciousness and Race Relations* (London, 1998), p. 290
[2] B. Ward, *Just My Soul Responding*, p.128; University of Newcastle Upon Tyne Oral History Collection, *Shelley Stewart interview with Brian Ward (*29/10/1995)
[3] B. Ward, *Just My Soul Responding*, p.128
[4] C. Werner, *A Change is Gonna Come: Music, Race and the Soul of America* (London, 1998), p.13

and those behind it, aided the community during the black freedom struggle in ways that scholars and the media have, through emphasising the voice of King and figure heads like him, unintentionally erased from mass public memory.[5] Being so focused on figure heads, no one thought of the power of music, and the collective identity it created for the black American community until many years later. No one understood, as Werner proclaims, the power and comfort music brought when, for example, bodies were being pulled out of the Mississippi river – unnamed and sometimes unrecognisable bodies of black men that would just become another tragic tale of segregationist violence in the South.[6] Ultimately, Soul and R&B music created a collective black identity that saw past the years of struggles and pain African Americans had endured and were going to experience for years to come. It was a sound that conjured up images of pride and excitement; it refused to allow the black community to succumb to the opinions, thoughts, and bigotry of many white Americans.[7]

However, it would be naïve to suggest that the only thing the emergence of black popular music did was create a black collective identity. The

---
[5] Ibid, p.4
[6] Ibid, p.8
[7] B. Ward, *Just My Soul Responding*, pp.243, 415

story of soul and rhythm and blues' power in the black fight for freedom strives deeper than that: it is a story of integration, 'complicated intertwining's of dirt poor roots and middle class dreams', the erosion of barriers and the projection of voices, the 'business ethic' and a story of hope.[8] It is about eroding not only barriers, but the legal restrictions and societal stigma of what it was to be black in America. It is the story of how music represents, and heavily influenced, a pivotal time in history. It shows how music knows no racial boundaries, and how the companies who created it affected the community in which they were set.

To fully understand music's role in the movement, it is important to understand the relationship between, and the origins of, rhythm and blues and soul. For most of the early post-war era until 1963, black and white music charts were separate; known pre-Second World War as race music, African American musical expression was over-looked and extremely marginalised.[9] However, Billboard magazine in an issue

---

[8] P. Guralnick, *Sweet Soul Music*, p.18
[9] A. Shaw, *Black Popular Music in America: From the Spirituals, Minstrels, and Ragtime to Soul, Disco and Hip-Hop* (New York, 1986), p.165; S. Tuck, *We Ain't What We Ought To Be: The Black Freedom Struggle From Emancipation to Obama* (Massachusetts, 2010), p.285

released on the 25th June 1949 coined the term R&B (rhythm and blues), and from then on the music industry used the term to describe most black music that didn't fit into gospel or blues styles.[10] The term R&B was used well into the sixties to describe the upbeat take on blues music that was not only evolving, but had become a staple of black America; 'viewed in musical terms' there was no reason why a sound originating and taking roots from the black American blues of Muddy Waters and B.B. King would become as popular and influential as it did.[11] But the circumstances, all racial, economic, and sociological of the post war era allowed the new evolving rhythm and blues music to flourish way until, and throughout, the 1960s.[12]

Involving the phenomenon that has been termed as 'shout singing', the electric guitar and the power of the tenor sax, the unpolished, unperfect and powerful sound that resonates in rhythm and blues is often deemed to be 'a more authentic or legitimate expression of black culture' than the soul genre that developed from it.[13] This is because rhythm and blues

---

[10] A. Shaw, *Black Popular Music in America*, p.165 & 'The Billboard The World's Foremost Amusement Weekly' *Billboard Magazine*, June 25, 1949, p.30
[11] A. Shaw, *Black Popular Music in America,* p.187
[12] Ibid, p.187
[13] A. Shaw, *Black Popular Music in America*, p.187; B. Ward, *Just My Soul Responding*, p.124

contained lyrics that strengthened the uniqueness of the black music form, by using distinctively black phrases like 'walk that walk... talk that talk... get down' and 'tell it like it is', and singing about real life experiences of black Americans - 'woke up hungry this morning... went down town to the grocery store and here's what the grocer said, where's my money?... My stomach is empty inside, I'm so hungry that I could die' – it was a testament to black American life and culture.[14] Eventually from R&B, Soul grew.[15]

More polished, more perfect, yet no less powerful, the sound that was soul music emerged in the early to mid-1960s. As Arnold Shaw represents 'if R&B singers were shouters, soul singers were screamers'; soul music's aim was to create an emotional response to the sound and lyrics that the artist projected.[16] Throughout the 1960s soul music overtook original rhythm and blues in expressing 'communal black feeling' and creating an African American consciousness that was known to the whole of America.[17] For the purpose of this thesis, I will

---

[14] B. Ward, *Just My Soul Responding,*, p.205, 210; W. Jones., *Where's My Money* (Peacock, 1963)
[15] M. Ellison, *Lyrical Protest: Black Music's Struggle Against Discrimination* (New York, 1989), p.4
[16] A. Shaw, *Black Popular Music in America*, pp.209, 211
[17] M. Ellison, *Lyrical Protest*, p.4

be using the phrases rhythm and blues (R&B) and soul music interchangeably to describe the whole of African American music from the years 1960-1972.

A conventional history involving the music styles of Rhythm and Blues and Soul would not be complete without the mention of the most famous soul and R&B music recording labels that ever existed, those labels called Motown and Stax.[18]

Figure 2 - Stax Record Company Logo

Figure 1 - Motown Record Company Logo

This thesis, therefore, is going to focus on their involvement within the community and the politically and socially motivated actions they proceeded in engaging with during the black freedom struggle. Therefore, it is important to understand the two labels and the differences between them.

---

[18] A. Shaw, *Black Popular Music in America*, p.217; Motown Museum (Online) Available at: www.motownmuseum.org; Stax Museum of American Soul Music (Online) Available at: https://staxmuseum.com/

Motown took inspiration for its sound from the church; powerful lead vocals, call and response aspects, hand clapping and its signature tambourine, all set it up to be one of the greatest sounds to come out of America.[19] It was mainly a sleek polished sound that every aspect of writing, recording, producing and selling was heavily controlled. It had the aim of appealing to, and reaching, both white and black America.[20] The Motown label was created and developed by Berry Gordy Jr in Detroit, Michigan in 1959. In contrast, Stax, the other label this writing will examine, was created by white brother and sister duo Jim Stewart (the St) and Estelle Axton (the ax) in 1957 in Memphis, Tennessee.[21] The sound Stax produced was unpolished and less controlled, partly because both Jim and Estelle knew very little about recording music, but mostly because 'feeling dictated the rhythm' and 'the pace' of many southern soul songs.[22] With no aim of appeasing white audiences, Stax and its artists accepted that even if the band was slightly out of tune, or 'the singer off key', a message could still be portrayed in its music.[23] It

---

[19] C. Werner, *A Change is Gonna Come,* p.19
[20] P. Guralnick, *Sweet Soul Music,* pp.7, 8
[21] S. E. Smith, *Dancing in the Street: Motown and the Cultural Politics of Detroit* (Massachusetts, 1999); Stax, *Stax History* (Online) Available at: www.staxrecords.com/history/
[22] P. Guralnick, *Sweet Soul Music,* p.8
[23] Ibid, p.8

was grittier, like original rhythm and blues, than the romanticised sounds coming from Gordy and his artists - no doubt this had something to do with the racism faced within the South of America that was less vicious in the North.[24] Arnold Shaw sums up perfectly the differences between the two labels and their styles - 'if Motown is the northern ghetto expanding into the white world of sleek automobiles' and polished pop, 'Stax is the Mississippi River overflowing the banks of the 1960s'. The sound Stax produced, deemed commonly as the Memphis sound, 'had more grit, gravel and mud in it'.[25]

By using this background knowledge, this writing is going prove that the black community, its collective identity, and the businesses within it show, how by working together and asserting itself, a community can go on to change the world in which it lives. It argues that economic advancement, and being treated equally, had major influence on the progress and success of the civil rights movement; by showing how the advancement of black media due to economic empowerment, and the opportunities provided by economic empowerment, influenced and benefited the black community. It illuminates how both businesses

---

[24] C. Werner, *A Change is Gonna Come*, p.56
[25] A. Shaw, *Black Popular Music in America*, p.218

managed to impact the community in which they were set despite time and place differences. Although there were different approaches to the community by both Motown and Stax, this writing proves that both impacted the community in which they were set, and both impacted the history of the place in which they called home. It also provides a history of Motown's involvement in the Great March to Freedom, something which impacted Detroit's history and its role in the civil rights movement and proves how the community as a collective is more powerful than any leader. It also provides a close history of Stax's role within the Memphis community, proving that Stax was for the black community rather than Motown being particularly aimed at white America.

Overall, both companies highlight a story of how black nationalist beliefs of economic empowerment allow community enhancement. By focusing on both Motown and Stax, it has also highlighted how black America, and it's fight for freedom, was all one despite which state one resonated in. It also argues that despite the focus on Motown being placed at the prime of the King years, and the focus on Stax residing in the beginning of the Black Power era that community empowerment is key to any revolution, and to both eras of the black freedom struggle.

The main contribution this writing will be adding to the scholarly work already on this topic, is the focus on overlooked sources, politically motivated gestures and productions by these companies. Consequently, it has placed Motown in relation to the black community in Detroit and shown how Gordy and his business helped the black community assert itself and recognise its needs, all socially, politically and economically. It has also provided the publication *Stax Fax* as a centre of attention, as this publication holds more significance than it is given credit. It has investigated how a monthly magazine can provide a community with an education about things that were not openly spoken about at the time, such as racism, abortion and sex. It has also shown that black media held a unique and significant role in the black community and has drawn conclusions surrounding Stax's involvement in the black community of Memphis, and how Stax provided not only opportunity but education through their many initiatives – something which has not been clearly investigated yet.

By looking at the two labels like this, one gets a story of how music and the people behind it created hope, opportunity and empowerment whilst also providing a collective identity. It can also be seen that small initiatives and actions can impact a community much greater than those actions undertaken by figureheads. It proves, what some have investigated through other case studies, that micro-histories and histories from below provide the true story of the black freedom struggle and that micro-histories in such a revolution are important to gain a better understanding of the movement and the people involved in it.[26] It also adds insight to the abundance of literature surrounding discussions of place and the civil rights movement, black empowerment in the sixties, comparative civil rights studies, the history of Detroit and Memphis, and the history of both Motown and Stax records.[27] It will also add insight to what some have investigated surrounding the Black Power movement; by focusing on Rev Cleage and other militant leaders in Detroit in relation to the Great March it will support other scholars in suggesting there was no sudden shift to a call for Black Power as has

---

[26] For scholarly work on history from below within the civil rights movement see especially - E. Crosby, *Civil Rights Struggles from the Ground Up: Local Struggles, a National Movement* (Georgia, Atlanta, 2011)

[27] For scholarly work on place and civil rights see especially - C. Lang, 'Locating the Civil Rights Movement: An Essay on the Deep South, Midwest, and Border South in Black Freedom Studies', *Journal of Social History 47.2* (2013); For scholarly work on black empowerment see especially - N. Batho, 'Black Power Children's Literature: Julius Lester and Black Power', *Journal of American Studies* (2019); For scholarly work on Memphis and Detroit in the civil rights movement see especially - J. T. Beifuss, *At the River I Stand: Memphis, the 1968 Strike and Martin Luther King* (New York, 1989); S. Fine, *Expanding the Frontiers of Civil Rights Michigan, 1948-1968* (Maryland, 2018)

been understood for many years.[28]

By doing all those things it also wishes to add to African American racial pride, knowledge and understanding, for as Marcus Garvey stated 'a people without the knowledge of their history, origin and culture is like a tree without roots'; it also hopes to prove to the modern generation that acceptance and understanding go a long way.[29]

There is an abundance of literature on the topic of music and the black freedom struggle. Susanne E Smith's book *Dancing in the Street: Motown and the Cultural Politics of Detroit* explores the relationship between Motown from the very beginning of its creation to the wider cultural politics of Detroit.[30] It exerts fascinating links between the two and shows that 'black newspapers, churches, radio stations and radio shows... poetry collectives and recording studios all worked... to articulate the needs of the... black community.'[31] Additionally, Anika

---

[28] S. Wendt, 'Protection or Path Toward Revolution?: Black Power and Self-Defense.' *Souls* (Colorado, 2007), p.320

[29] D. Marley, & Nas., *Distant Relatives* (Def Jam Recordings, 2010); Black History Month, *Marcus Garvey Famously Wrote* (2020) (Online) Available at: https://www.blackhistorymonth.org.uk/article/section/bhm-intros/marcus-garvey-famously-wrote-a-people%E2%80%AFwithout%E2%80%AFknowledge-of-their-past-history-origin-and-culture-is-like-a%E2%80%AFtree-without-roots/

[30] S. E. Smith, *Dancing in the Street*
[31] Ibid, p.8

Boyce's account of Motown and its direct relationship with the civil rights movement focuses on message music, Motown's Black Forum label and other politically overt acts of Motown. In doing so she shows links between the label and the wider picture of race relations in America.[32]

Charles Hughes has shown how the Stax label promoting 'their recordings of symbols of integrationism' allowed the label to become 'pivotal actors in the larger trajectory of US racial politics in the twentieth century.'[33] Guralnick's *Sweet Soul Music* is also a detailed read surrounding music and race relations in the South. He centres on the Stax recording label as an entity of relationships and community.[34] Guralnick has argued that southern soul music was 'a kind of revolutionary statement', that mirrored the ongoing fight for integration and freedom.[35]

Furthermore, additional writings on Stax and Motown include Robert Gordon's *Respect Yourself* that links the history of the civil rights

---

[32] A.K. Boyce, "What's Going On": Motown and the Civil Rights Movement (Boston, Massachusetts, 2008)
[33] C. L. Hughes, *Country Soul: Making Music and Making Race in the American South* (Chapel Hill, North Carolina, 2015), p.3
[34] P. Guralnick, *Sweet Soul Music*
[35] Ibid, p.4

movement to the development and ongoings of Stax records and has proved to be very useful in relation to this project.[36] Whilst Bowman adds to the literature on the topic with a detailed history of Stax.[37] Other influential writings surrounding Motown include both George's and Waller's descriptive accounts of the company's history.[38] Both Ward and Werner's books have proven to be a detailed account of soul music in both the north and south of America. Ward's *Just My Soul Responding* expresses the links between black music's ever-growing fame and a growing black consciousness in mid-twentieth century America.[39] It links music, its artists and studios to the ever-developing position of black Americans and places it in context of race relations of the sixties and seventies.

Additionally, Werner provides a fascinating insight into black music's role in social history of both America and the world throughout the twentieth century.[40]

Others, such as Shaw's *Black Popular Music in America,* address the

---

[36] R. Gordon, *Respect Yourself: Stax records and the Soul Explosion* (New York, 2013)
[37] R. Bowman, *Soulsville, USA: The story of Stax Records* (New York, 1997)
[38] N. George, *Where Did Our Love Go?: The Rise & Fall of the Motown Sound* (London, 2003), D. Waller, *The Motown Story* (New York, 1985)
[39] B. Ward, *Just My Soul Responding*
[40] C. Werner, *A Change is Gonna Come*

role of music in African American culture more generally, and how not only this relationship between community and music developed but also how African American music has developed from 'the spirituals' to 'Hip-Hop.'[41]

As noted above there has been a small number of scholars who have investigated the relationship of soul and rhythm and blues and the black freedom struggle. This writing is specifically going to focus on the two labels of Motown and Stax as businesses, communities and media producers.

Firstly, by focusing on the Motown label this dissertation has explored how Motown's spoken word recording of King's Great March to Freedom speech, proves how black business and media can unite the black community and help it assert itself; proving that the community was at the heart of the black freedom struggle. It has placed the album into the context of the Northern freedom movement and shown that the movement in Detroit was in as much need as the movement in the South. It has also explored how the creation and success of black capitalism by Gordy generated hope and inspiration for most African Americans. It

---

[41] A. Shaw, *Black Popular Music in America*

has proven black nationalist philosophies work to empower the community economically which leads to social and political advancement. Additionally, it has proven that once you give a community the means to become economically sufficient it can change the course of the future. It has also proven that Motown held a powerful place in American culture during the mid-twentieth century; it acknowledges Motown's political subsidiary label 'Black Forum' and proves how music could break down not only cultural barriers but also racial ones; showing that Motown's appeal to white America was one of the most important parts a black business played in the black freedom struggle.

Then, using Stax as a case study, this writing reiterates how integration in the Stax recording, publishing, and song writing community provided proof that white and black America could live together and thrive.[42] It also focuses on the racial advancement and greater opportunities music provided African Americans in the South, showing how it helped to change race relations. It has shown how Stax's involvement in the community supported the black freedom struggle through their

---

[42] C. L. Hughes, *Country Soul*; P. Guralnick, *Sweet Soul Music*

educational monthly magazine called *Stax Fax*. Stax helped to get the community politically active and enhance community and racial pride through this publication and this is something that has not been analysed or the centre of scholarship before. It will closely analyse the contents of this publication and place it in context to the civil rights movement, the fight for freedom in Memphis and its community.

The primary sources used range widely from magazines, posters, advertisements, newspapers, oral histories, interviews, testaments from groups such as CORE, SNCC and the White Citizens Council, and simply the music these companies produced. Reading many scholars work, I have been able to decipher which sources to be cautious of and which would best suit my project. This writing has found that including sources that show the public dimension of the story such as the magazines *Billboard* and *Cash Box*, and other media that was predominantly black, has helped to convey a story of how the community were affected by both Motown and Stax in more ways than just listening and buying their music.[43] Although there is caution

---

[43] *Billboard Magazine 1894 – 2017* (Online) Available at: https://worldradiohistory.com/Archive-All-Music/Billboard-Magazine.htm; *Cash Box Magazine 1942 – 1996* (Online) Available at: https://worldradiohistory.com/Archive-All-Music/Cash-Box-Magazine.htm - I would also like to thank Charles Hughes for pointing me in the direction of Cash Box

surrounding autobiographies, they have provided detailed accounts of how artists saw the labels and how artists saw racism and the movement more generally through their eyes and memory. The limitations of travel have impacted this book slightly, as I have not been able to consult certain collections of newspapers and archives as I would have liked. However, the reading of over one hundred scholars' work and the consultation of the online archives and collection are sufficient to make a good judgement of the role of Motown and Stax within the black freedom struggle.

Additionally, there has been, in some studies, a heavy reliance on song lyrics of proof for soul and rhythm and blues' voice in the black fight for freedom, which, as Ward suggests, can cause problems, and show naivety in a way that suggests one does not fully understand the other influences music had on the black freedom struggle. Many, if not most, movement historians often touch upon songs like James Brown's 'Say it Loud (I'm Black and I'm Proud)' as proof of soul music's political and sociological engagement with the black fight for freedom.[44]

Magazine as it has been of immense use and has provided great insight to this research.
[44] B. Ward, *Just My Soul Responding*, p.20

Additionally, and not surprisingly, many of these historians fail to draw attention to the fact the song was released in 1968, a year which was well embedded into the fight for freedom. Showing soul and R&B's power in the movement as miniscule especially as the movement was 'more than a dozen years old' by the time that song was released.[45] There has also been a lot of focus on political masking within songs and lyrics. When Ben E. King harmoniously calls out 'I won't be afraid, no I won't be afraid, just as long as you stand by me', to the public he is speaking to a lover, but to the black community he was speaking to the Lord. If you imagine the song being in the mind of a black person walking on a dark 'southern back road', the song's deeper meaning seems obvious.[46] The example of Martha Reeves & the Vandellas 'Dancing in the Street' has come up time after time whilst I have been undertaking this research - 'summers here, the time is right, for dancing in the street'. Many took the song as an outcry for summer riots especially as dance 'represented action and initiative.'[47] In 1965, Edwin Starr's release 'Back Street' for Ric-Tic, a Motown subsidiary, actually

---

[45] B. Ward, *Just My Soul Responding*, p.290; J. Brown, *Say it Loud (I'm Black and I'm Proud)* (King, 1968)
[46] C. Werner, *A Change is Gonna Come*, p.36; B. E. King, *Stand By Me* (Atco, 1961)
[47] B. Ward, *Just My Soul Responding*, p.210; M. Reeves & The Vandellas, *Dancing in the Street* (Gordy, 1964)

'represented a careful mythologisation of the ghetto', explaining 'I've been living on the main street where society is the thing... Although I live on main street, the back street is where I belong... Where people stick together, one for all and all for one'; he shows that even though he was a black man who had managed to break away from the holds of the ghetto he knew that it would always be his home and offer him a sense of belonging.[48] The list could go on, and it would be very extensive. I am not dismissing political masking in lyrics, and I am not saying political masking was not common and was not important. It certainly was, but I feel that those writings have been exhausted enough and I do not want to attempt to retell the knowledge or importance of political masking.

***

When Booker T wrote that on 'one Saturday morning when I was nine years old, my dad told me... "Go back in the house and get your clarinet. We're going to get a haircut."' And once he started playing, 'the shop quieted... The tune I picked up was a very popular song... the men recognised the tune instantly', he proves how music would unite, is the

---

[48] B. Ward, *Just My Soul Responding*, p.215; E. Starr, *Back Street* (Ric-Tic, 1966)

heart of the community and is a mutual interest we all have despite race, age or belief.[49] His retelling clearly shows that music was at the centre of community.

The story this writing will project is one, as I will credit Werner for saying, 'of how music radiates healing energies', how black music of all kinds has helped us throughout history to 'imagine a world where we can get along, without turning off our minds.'[50] It has proven what Martin Luther King explained, that rhythm and blues and soul music 'paved the way for social and political change by creating a powerful, cultural bridge'.[51] This writing is going to focus on the 'public dimension of the story'.[52] It is going to show that 'music's potential as a liberating force exists in constant dialogue' and that rhythm and blues and soul music essentially 'changed the world.'[53]

---

[49] B. T. Jones, *Time is Tight: My Life, Note by Note* (New York, 2017), pp.13, 14

[50] C. Werner, *A Change is Gonna Come*, p.xiii
[51] B. Ward, *Just My Soul Responding*, p.232
[52] C. Werner, *A Change is Gonna Come*, p.xv
[53] C. L. Hughes, *Country Soul*, p.193

'Ain't no place like Motown, Hitsville U.S.A': Community, Political Expression, Black Capitalism, and 'The Sound of Young America'[54]

---

[54] Black History Month, *Motown at 60... A Legacy To Be Remembered* (2020) (Online) Available at: https://www.blackhistorymonth.org.uk/article/section/music-entertainers/motown-at-60-a-legacy-to-be-remembered/

Figure 3 - View of men working on Ford cars assembly line

Before the twentieth century, Detroit had always been a place unlike the rest of America. Tales of the Underground Railroad and the road to freedom from slavery echo in its past, and from the 1920s a new road to freedom from poverty, from Jim Crow, and from little opportunity, began to be shouted from Detroit's streets.[55]

African Americans were attracted to Detroit because of the opportunities the city presented. With the five dollar a day wage announcement in 1914, Ford Motors provided employment and opportunity in Detroit that was so unlike African American

---

[55] N. George, *Where Did Our Love Go?*, p.8

opportunities in the South.[56] In Blues People, Amiri Baraka (LeRoi Jones) - a black cultural leader who is well known for his poetry, essays and music analysis'- states that not only did 'Ford become synonymous with Northern opportunity', but their 'Model-T was one of the first automobiles Negroes could purchase.'[57]

In Detroit particularly, blues music travelled with the Southern blacks that migrated north in the earliest part of the twentieth century. Blues and similar music provided a creative break from Ford's assembly lines but rarely an opportunity for employment or greater success.[58] It was not until the social and political climate began to change in America that recording and singing black music emerged as a method to become successful, and the creation of Motown Records by Berry Gordy Jr in 1959 proved this.

---

[56] N. George, *Where Did Our Love Go?*, p.9; S. E. Smith, *Dancing in the Street*, p.12
[57] A. Baraka, *Blues People: Negro Music in White America* (1980), p.97; Detroit Public Library Digital Collections, *Ford automobiles on assembly line* (Online) Available at: https://digitalcollections.detroitpubliclibrary.org/islandora/object/islandora%3A186522
[58] S. E. Smith, *Dancing in the Street*, p.13

Figure 4 - Berry Gordy outside Motown Recording Studios 'Hitsville USA'

Gordy Senior left Georgia because his business was receiving hostile attention as it was deemed too successful. Unbeknownst at the time Berry Gordy would go on to create the most successful black business to ever exist, but he would not receive the hostility his father once did.[59]

***

Relatively, Detroit was a quiet city, but the creation of Motown's recording studio at 2648 West Grand Boulevard radiated a sound and a success that should not be seen as separate to the intertwining's of the

---

[59] Ibid, p.62

'hum of factory machinery', and the social change and political awakenings that were taking place during the sixties in Detroit.[60] When the Velvelettes sing 'ain't no place like Motown, Hitsville, USA' in the single ('Ain't No Place Like Motown') that was rediscovered and released in 2002, they certainly spoke words of truth.[61] The song praises the uniqueness of the Motown recording studio and the sound that it produced, but the lyrics represent the exceptionality of Detroit, also known as the Motor City or Motown, as a community, as an enterprise and as a hub for black advancement and prosperity. The creation of Motown Records in 1959 exceeded 'all previous expectations' of a black business and it has been argued, notably by Smith, that it could not have happened anywhere but Detroit.[62] There was certainly no other place like Motown, both city and recording studio, and the circumstances in Detroit and the place that it held during the decade of the sixties allowed Motown Records and black cultural expression to thrive.

---

[60] A.K. Boyce, *"What's Going On"*, p.30; S. E. Smith, *Dancing in the Street,* pp.5, 19; Wayne State University Libraries, *Motown Record Corporation; Exterior of Hitsville, U.S.A* (Online) Available at: https://digital.library.wayne.edu/item/wayne:vmc52439

[61] Motown, Tamla Motown, Universal., 'Ain't No Place Like Motown', *A Cellarful Of Motown* (Album, 2002)

[62] A.K. Boyce, *"What's Going On"*, p. 79; S. E. Smith, *Dancing in the Street,* p.8

During the sixties, with the advancement of the civil rights movement, any form of 'black cultural expression', whether that be literature, poetry, radio, or music, had the energy to be considered political or within a political context even if it was not; and Motown Records was no exception.[63] Motown soon discovered if a song was sung by a black person, produced by a black person, or promoted by a black person, no matter how un-politically motivated, it would 'be implicated in the racial politics of the time.'[64]

Motown was a hit factory, and that is why it is best known as Hitsville, USA. It is a well-known fact that Gordy had a Ford assembly line inspired process to produce Motown's music. Soon this production method would lead to the creation of the Motown Sound, a sound that is still recognisable to this day. The perfection of the sound was not only in the way the lyrics were written or the instruments that were played, but it was also in the way in which the artists were portrayed to America – they had to be 'perfect and poised in their dress, talk and dance.'[65] Motown artists were black, and that meant having to put in extra effort

---

[63] S. E. Smith, *Dancing in the Street*, p.136
[64] Ibid, pp.5, 172
[65] A.K. Boyce, *"What's Going On"*, pp. 30, 41

to appease racist stereo types and gain success in wider America. Motown used the industrial strategies of Detroit's wider industry, namely Ford, to create African American music that exceeded racist stereotypes, an 'Afro American music without apology, by Afro American artists who project vibrant dignity.'[66]

Producing artists such as The Supremes, Marvin Gaye and Stevie Wonder, and having its first number one in 1961, Motown produced a symbol of black pride when those symbols were not readily available.[67] Not only do the cultural politics of Detroit show that in the right set of circumstances anything is possible, they show that 'social, cultural, economic and political change emerges from distinct communities'.[68] As Motown artist Smokey Robinson explains, even if somewhat nostalgically, 'the Motown sound was a miracle… it was black music too damn good – too accessible, too danceable' and 'too real – not to be loved by everyone.'[69]

---

[66] A.K. Boyce, *"What's Going On"*, p.72; S. E. Smith, *Dancing in the Street,* p.141
[67] S. E. Smith, *Dancing in the Street*, p.6
[68] Ibid, p.259
[69] S. Robinson, *Smokey: Inside My Life* (London, 2017), p.137

Motown and the Black Community's 'Great March to Freedom'

It is no surprise that during the sixties, when the call for equal rights was prominent, that racial politics would become more complicated and complex.[70] African Americans were finally allowed to start 'negotiating new definitions of self and collective identity', which not only aided racial pride but began to effectively change race relations throughout America.[71] Many civil rights and black freedom struggle scholars have ignored, undermined or struggled to understand the role black music played in the fight for freedom; they often seek a direct link between artists and their role in using their voices to impact America.[72] Therefore, as Boyce expresses, many disregard the role Motown played in the early civil rights movement because of the lack of message songs or politically motivated music, and many argue Motown could and should have done more to aid the black fight for freedom.[73] Not only does this idea hold itself in racist rhetoric – adding extra pressure on Motown to get politically engaged just because it was a black business,

---

[70] B. Ward, *Just My Soul Responding,* p.166
[71] Ibid, p.166
[72] Ibid, p.291
[73] A.K. Boyce, *"What's Going On",* p.75

something that would have not been expected by a white business doing the same thing as Motown, simply recording music – it also undermines Motown's involvement in the black freedom struggle.[74] Yet Motown provided the soundtrack to a whole era, and even if Gordy was reluctant to engage with politics on his main labels, he did record political recordings, create a subsidiary label and he eventually allowed some of his artists to project their voices through message music; indeed, Motown greatly influenced the black freedom struggle.[75] Motown's music was always prominent in the 1960s in many ways, one of the most famous campaigns Gordy permitted his artists to perform at was the Poor People's Campaign in 1968. It was a 'racially, geographically and politically diverse' group of poor people, who protested 'the unseen poverty they suffered on a daily basis.'[76]

---

[74] Ibid, p.75
[75] S.E. Smith, *Dancing in the Street*, p.20
[76] A. N. Wright, 'The 1968 Poor People's Campaign, Marks, Mississippi, and the Mule Train: Fighting Poverty Locally, Representing Poverty Nationally' in E. Crosby, *Civil Rights History From The Ground Up: Local Struggles, A National Movement'* (Georgia, Atlanta, 2011). p.110; Civil Rights Digital Library, *Series of WSB-TV news film clips of African Americans celebrating and demonstrating as they prepare for the Poor People's March on Washington* (1968) (Online) Available at: http://crdl.usg.edu/cgi/crdl?format=_video;query=id:ugabma_wsbn_wsbn44591; D. A. Ellis (Motown Museum)., *Atlanta Journal 'Songs Give Poor Marchers Life After Day of Waiting'* (1968) Available by request; D. A, Ellis, (Motown Museum)., *Jet Magazine 'Motown Stars Raise $25,000 For Poor Campaign'* (1968) Available by request

Motown Stars Raise $25,000 For Poor Campaign

The Poor People's Campaign was getting set to leave Atlanta, and march leaders, after huddling, became alarmed over the shortage of funds. Mrs. Martin Luther King Jr., who was recently elected to the board of directors of the march-sponsoring Southern Christian Leadership Conference, put in a hurry-up call to an old friend and supporter, dynamic Berry Gordy, president of the Detroit-based Motown Recording Co. As a result, in less than 24 hours, Gordy had canceled scheduled appearances of his stars—Diana Ross and The Supremes, The Temptations, Stevie Wonder, Gladys Knight and The Pips, Chuck Jackson and Yvonne Fair—to stage a huge benefit rally at the 10,000-seat New Atlanta Auditorium. More than 13,000—3,000 over the limit—jammed the auditorium and added more than $25,000 to the Poor People's Campaign till. Gordy not only diverted some of his top stars to the benefit rally, but he flew in from New York with an 11-piece Motown band to accompany his stars. The Atlanta campaign was jointly sponsored by the Metropolitan Atlanta Summit Leadership Congress and the SCLC. Earlier in the evening before the concert, Gordy, with Mrs. King and recording artists, unveiled a plaque marking Dr. King's birthplace in Atlanta just two blocks from Ebenezer Baptist Church. Dr. King co-pastored the church with his father, the Rev. Martin Luther King Sr.

Figure 5 - Motown Stars Raise $25,000 For Poor Campaign. Jet Magazine, 23/5/1968

It is important to emphasise that African Americans of the time assigned both 'political and cultural meanings' to their music despite whether the artists or label were actively engaged in the fight for civil rights and freedom.[77] Throughout the whole of Motown's popularity Gordy was reluctant to engage in political conversation and steer away from his dream to create and produce music. The most Motown's singers initially did was perform at speeches or marches, often drawing the crowds, and then 'were made to feel like an afterthought.'[78] Even in the late sixties

---

[77] B., Ward, *Just My Soul Responding*, p.187
[78] Ibid, p.328

Gordy was reluctant to allow his artists to engage with political conversation. On one occasion Jackson 5 were asked whether they supported Black Power philosophies. Before any of the group could answer, a Motown spokesperson interrupted the interviewer and expressed that the group were a 'commercial product' and thus had no opinions on the matter.[79]

Detroit was an extremely politically aware city during the 1960s. Despite hopes of less discrimination and racism, many blacks who migrated from the South learnt that the North was 'more troubled… than they had been led to believe'.[80] Blacks faced 'growing restrictions', police brutality, a housing crisis, and unemployment in Northern cities.[81] Alongside all of these aspects that proved Detroit was far from the model city it was named to be, educational discrimination proved that Southern blacks hopes of equal education above the Mason-Dixon Line was just that, a hope.[82] Additionally, clashes between activist groups such as the NAACP and more militant leaders such as Malcolm X and the Freedom Now Party made the freedom movement in Detroit

---

[79] S.E. Smith, *Dancing in the Street*, p.229
[80] T. J. Sugrue, *Sweet Land of Liberty: The Forgotten Struggle for Civil Rights in the North* (New York, 2009), pp, xx, xxi, 6
[81] Ibid, p.259
[82] Ibid, p.171

tense and somewhat divided.[83] It is no wonder why Gordy did not want his company involved in the politics of Detroit, or favouring certain beliefs over others. However, on August 28th, 1963, Motown released its first political spoken word album on its subsidiary label 'Gordy'.

Figure 7 - Motown's 'The Great March to Freedom' album

Figure 6 - Motown's Great March To Freedom Album

Entitled 'The Great March to Freedom', the recording was of Martin Luther King's speech at the march split into smaller sections. The speech included a rehearsal of his 'I Have a Dream' speech which he recited months later at the Great March on Washington.[84] The album was more than just a recording of an emerging Martin Luther King Jr;

---

[83] T. J. Sugrue, *Sweet Land of Liberty*, p.299; S.E. Smith, *Dancing in the Street*, p.92
[84] Ibid, p.21

it 'marked a critical juncture in the history of Motown Records' and it was their first attempt to place themselves in the wider landscape of the fight for racial justice.[85] The album was purposefully released on the same date King marched on Washington, commemorating 'King's appearance in Detroit two months earlier.'[86]

King's appearance in Detroit gave Detroit's black community the chance to support Southern African Americans in the struggle for freedom by raising funds for the SCLC's (Southern Christian Leadership Conference) Birmingham campaign.[87] By initiating over 125,000 to march down Woodward Avenue, notably the dividing line between the black and white communities in Detroit, it allowed the black community to assert their needs as a collective body.[88] King's speech that day in June highlighted to the black Detroit community that not only was racism, segregation and violence a problem in the Southern states but all of those things held a significant

---

[85] Ibid, p.21
[86] S.E. Smith, *Dancing in the Street*, p.21; Detroit Historical Society, *The Great March to Freedom* (Online) Available at: https://detroithistorical.pastperfectonline.com/archive/E8BD6C51-A7C8-44B9-A033-254882954020
[87] S.E. Smith, *Dancing in the Street*, p.23
[88] S.E. Smith, *Dancing in the Street*, pp.23, 37; D. A. Ellis, (Motown Museum)., *Official Programme Front Cover of the Walk to Freedom March* (1963) Available by request

place within the black community of the north – particularly Detroit. Not legally but as King explained 'it exists in three areas, in the area of employment discrimination, in the area of housing discrimination, and in the area of de facto segregation in public schools.'[89] Speaking of how the plantation way of life was beginning to fail because the black community now had the choice to move around America, King emphasised the importance of the black community and its white allies in the fight for freedom. The mention of white allies makes the speech less militant, and slightly more conciliatory, than others who were speaking in Detroit around the same time such as Malcolm X. Urging the black community in Detroit to help the black community 'down in Alabama, Mississippi, all over the south…' King empahisesd Detroit's citizens needed 'to work with determination to get rid of any segregation and discrimination in Detroit. Realising that injustice anyhwere is a threat to justice everywhere.'[90] The *Detroit Free Press*, one of the longest lasting and popular newspapers in circulation in Detroit,

---

[89] M. L. King, *Great March to Freedom Rally Speech* (1963) Online (Available at: https://www.youtube.com/watch?v=0aO7mXbx2lo)
[90] Ibid

described the March as 'a tremendous expression of the Negro community's determination.'[91]

Figure 8 - Martin Luther King Jr leading the march

---

[91] J., Mann, *'Negroes Here Pledge More Demonstrations'* Detroit Free Press (June, 1963)
[92] Wayne State University Libraries, *King, Martin Luther; Negro Leader – Freedom Parade* (1963) (Online) Available at: https://digital.library.wayne.edu/item/wayne:vmc53524_2; D. A. Ellis, (Motown Museum)., Aerial *Photograph of Freedom March* (1963) Available by request

Figure 9 - Detroit Free Press, 125,000 Walk Quietly in Record Rights Plea (24/6/1963)

Figure 10 - Thousands march down Woodward Avenue

Figure 11 - Front cover of The Illustrated News pamphlet on the Great March to Freedom

The Illustrated News, written by Albert Cleage a black nationalist, in their June 1963 issue also show how the cooperation of black businesses to promote freedom protests was extremely influential to the gains of the black freedom struggle. This issue promoted invovlement in the March, and similarly to Motown's Great March to Freedom album, preserved the impact of King's march in Detroit, his aims and the collective power of Detroit's black community.

The issue gave details of the the march, including instructions on where to meet, and how those within the community who want to take part in the march should organise.[94] As Sugrue explains, the fact that a militant voice such as Cleage was heavily involved in the march proves the diversity of the 'northern freedom struggle. Additonally, the fact that 'the recognition by organisers that the Great March would not be legitimate if it did not contain miilitant voices' also proves this.[95] The Illustrated News was influential in asserting the black community in realtion to this march and the problems African Americans were facing in Detroit; Cleage saw the Great March as an opportunity to create solidarity amongst the black community.[96] One article in the magazine by Rev Albert B Cleage Jr entitled 'We Shall Overcome' expresses the importance of protest within the black community - 'if the pressure of the Negro protest is removed, our movement towards first class citizenship will stop!' The article goes on to explain that 'the walls of segregation and discrimination are crumbling because of the increasing pressure of Negro Protest' and shows just how important the community

---

[94] Rise Up North Detroit, *"We Shall Overcome" by Reverend Albert B. Cleage* (1963) (Online) Available at: https://riseupdetroit.org/wp-content/uploads/2019/02/We-Shall-Overcome_.pdf?iframe=true&width=100%&height=100%
[95] T. J. Sugrue, *Sweet Land of Liberty*, p.301
[96] Ibid, p.299

were in the fight for freedom, particualrly as the article recognises times were changing and different things needed to be done to move with the changing fight; 'The NAACP has become 'one among many' rather than "the one" in our Civil Rights struggle… it cannot… hope to supplant Rev Martin Luther King, Core and Snick no matter how loudly Roy Wilkins screams about the importance of the NAACP.' It also echoes the on going battle between the NAACP and black nationlists on who should be at the centre of the movement, and who should take control of it. There was continuous contraversy surrounding the role of the NAACP and in the early years of the movement. During the Second World War era, it can be argued the NAACP were already not acting 'effectively in the… working-class neighbourhoods where black Americans fought their most decisive decisions.'[97] It has been noted by Thomas Sugrue, that the Detroit branch of the NAACP initally refused to support the Great March 'unless white liberals… were given prominent billing.' Reverend C. L. Franklin (father of Aretha), the coordinator of the march, highlighted the divisions between activists groups in Detroit further, claiming members of the NAACP were a

---

[97] R. Korstad, & N. Lichtenstein, 'Opportunities Found and Lost: Labour, Radicals, and the Early Civil Rights Movement', *Journal of American History 75.3* (1988), p.787

'bunch of Toms' (a person described as an Uncle Tom or Tom is often seen as being submissive and obedient to white people).[98] Not only does this article make the community politically and socially aware, it also assures them of their importance within the movement.[99] This edition of the Illustrated News also inlcudes information on other ways the black community in Detroit can support the black fight for freedom. On page five a bold title reads '"Do not buy where you cannot work!" Support… campaigns against A&P food stores sponsored by preachers of Detroit & vicinity against Kroger Markets sponsored by CORE'. The words 'united for freedom' are then written at the bottom, proving that many understood the only way African Americans were going to win the fight for freedom was by being united.[100] This edition also supported voting rights campaigns and urged the people reading to 'register to vote'.[101]

---

[98] T. J. Sugrue, *Sweet Land of Liberty*, p.299
[99] Rise Up North Detroit, *"We Shall Overcome" by Reverend Albert B. Cleage* (1963)
[100] Ibid
[101] Ibid

Figure 12 - Page 5 of the Illustrated News June 1963 edition

Figure 13 - Official Programme for the 'Great March to Freedom'

The march showed the collective power of Detroit's black community and through its recording Motown preserved this collective power forever and helped to aid the fight for freedom in the years following the Great March with the album. The album preserved King's voice in a way that other historical figures before him had not had the chance.[102] The Illustrated News stands as a testimony to how politically engaged the black community in Detroit were, and how the black businesses of Detroit came together in times of need to speak up and preserve a voice

---

[102] S.E. Smith, *Dancing in the Street*, p.37

for future generations.

The new ability of being able to use media as a tool to aid the fight for freedom was becoming understood in the sixties.[103] Not only did black Detroit use local radio stations, newspapers, and magazines to assert a sense of community but they used the political recordings of Motown, like this one, to teach, exemplify, and raise awareness around the injustices the black community faced. The album was also used to show how grassroots, organised protest, policies and laws were emerging to tackle them.[104] Ultimately, Motown's recording of King's initial speech at the Great March to Freedom was the first way the company publicly engaged with the political thought of the time, and the recording preserved King's speech for generations to come.[105] The album initiated solidarity between Motown and the black community within Detroit and across America, showing that Motown was more than a musical entity, had concious thought and stood with the importance of the black freedom struggle. The fact that black businesses such as Motown and The Illustrated News came together to not only promote the march, but support King and the black freedom struggle, shows how the collective

---

[103] Ibid, p.37
[104] Ibid, p.37
[105] Ibid, p.92

power of the black community, its businesses and its media can have an immense impact on the preserving of black history and the making of it.

Money (That's What I Want) – Black Capitalism and Community Empowerment

Released in 1959, Barrett Strong's single 'Money (That's What I Want)' only held a glimpse of the success Berry Gordy would achieve owning Motown Records. Reaching number two on *Billboards* R&B chart, the song echoed much of the desires and needs of the black community throughout Detroit, but little did Gordy know that it would be the first record of many that would lead Motown to be a multi-million-dollar business.[106]

Black culture had always been important in the fight for civil rights. From freedom songs to photographs, black culture and its media educated many about the everlasting racial injustices that existed in America. As Tuck mentions 'Detroit's vibrant black music scene was a reminder that African Americans fought for freedom in culture as well as politics.[107]

As John Lewis expressed, the early days of the civil rights movement were fuelled by people 'singing songs that came straight from their soul,

---

[106] S. E. Smith, *Dancing in the Street*, p.76
[107] Ibid, pp.92, 93; S., Tuck, *We Ain't What We Ought To Be*

with words they felt in every bone of their body'; many early protests show the community coming together to sing freedom songs.[108] In Detroit the development of black culture as a tool would become increasingly important in not only the city's fight for civil rights but the wider fight across America. Particularly the importance of radio stations, and what they projected into the black community, held significance in the black fight for freedom. As James Farmer, director of CORE, expressed 'all radio stations that beam to the black community… must take responsibility to that community' – similarly as grassroots protests held importance in the community, so did the black media.[109] Motown's relationship to the black community also provided opportunities for black capitalism to thrive and empowered a black commerce in Detroit which impacted the whole of America.[110] Of course, the most obvious argument here is that Berry Gordy was a black man who owned a black business that projected black people, and

---

[108] J. Lewis, *Walking with the Wind: a Memoir of the Movement* (New York, 1998), p. 22; Civil Rights Library of St Augustine, *Singing Freedom Songs* (1964) (Online) Available at: https://cdm16000.contentdm.oclc.org/digital/collection/p16000coll3/id/76

[109] Cash Box Magazine, *NATRA, 'New Deejay Responsibilities', Farmer, Others Speak* (30/8/1969) (Online) Available at: https://worldradiohistory.com/hd2/IDX-Business/Music/Archive-Cash-Box-IDX/60s/1969/CB-1969-08-30-OCR-Page-0033.pdf#search=%22black%20power%22

[110] S. E. Smith, *Dancing in the Street*, p.9

their music, across the United States and eventually the world. This was not only inspiring but also empowering to African Americans across America; in the South segregation and racism were still very prominent and the fact that Motown and its artists were very much proving that black people 'had the potential to go far beyond successful to superstardom' inspired and gave hope to many.[111] But the founding of Motown and its role as a black business in the community goes far beyond inspiration and empowerment.[112] Motown came to be the most successful black 'cultural producer and eventually the country's most successful black business', and this is something that cannot be excluded from political discussion of the time.[113]

---

[111] A.K. Boyce, *"What's Going On"*, p.48
[112] Wayne State University Libraries, *Gordy, Berry Jr.; President Motown Records* (Online) Available at: https://digital.library.wayne.edu/item/wayne:vmc26608
[113] S. E. Smith, *Dancing in the Street*, p.11

Figure 14 - Berry Gordy with numerous Motown albums

Motown was essentially built on the very principles that the civil rights and Black Power movements were built on, most notably 'black empowerment, economic uplift [and] equality.'[114] The teachings of Booker T Washington were central to Gordy and his founding of Motown. The philosophy of Washington's 'economic self-sufficiency' was well engrained in not only the founding of Motown but many other black businesses in Detroit.[115] Washington understood that the government policy of laissez faire in America was not discriminatory towards the African American community generally, but that society kept the black community from achieving economic success and

---

[114] A.K. Boyce, *"What's Going On"*, p.47
[115] S. E. Smith, *Dancing in the Street,* p.55; Tuskegee University, *Dr. Booker Taliaferro Washington* (2021) (Online) Available at: https://www.tuskegee.edu/discover-tu/tu-presidents/booker-t-washington

independence. The only way the African American community could achieve equal status and have power within society was through capitalism and economic advancement.[116] This was also something Malcolm X believed in, and economic empowerment was readily prominent in many aspects of the civil rights movement. Malcolm X stressed that African Americans could not 'stabilise their own community' until they stopped relying on white owned businesses for their economic welfare, rather, they needed to create their own business which would lead to a well-established emergence of black capitalism. Which thus over time would not only stabilise but improve the black community. Ultimately, this would empower the black community by taking the control of their success and wealth from white America.[117] Martin Luther King Jr openly acknowledged that discrimination had its many forms in the North, as it did in the South, despite Detroit being labelled as a model city for race relations.[118] Blacks who moved to Detroit had their hopes dashed when they noticed the 'enormous gap in affluence, status and power between themselves and whites.'[119]

---

[116] A.K. Boyce, *"What's Going On"*, p.48
[117] A.K. Boyce, *"What's Going On"*, p.50
[118] S. E. Smith, *Dancing in the Street*, p.25
[119] T. J. Sugrue, *Sweet Land of Liberty*, p.257

Gordy's economic advancement and the economic opportunities he provided the black community in Detroit directly fought racial discrimination. King expressed in the first rendition of his 'I Have a Dream' speech that 'right here in Detroit a Negro will be able to buy a house or rent a house anywhere that their money will carry them.'[120] Essentially, Motown proved these philosophies and influenced Kings hopes. Gordy empowered Detroit's black community through his economic independence and success by creating opportunities for the black community that were not previously available. As Mary Wilson of The Supremes acknowledged 'until Motown, in Detroit, there were three big careers for a black girl: babies, the factories or day work...' and for men Ford and similar assembly line industries provided most employment.[121] Within the aspects of black capitalism, commerce and economic success, Motown proved that black capitalism could be 'a tool in the fight for racial justice'; it provided hope, empowerment and opportunities and improved the economics of Detroit's black neighbourhood.[122] Even organisers of Detroit's famous Freedom Now

---

[120] S. E. Smith, *Dancing in the Street*, p.31; WNYC, *Deconstructing Martin Luther King Jr's Dream* (2013) (Online) Available at: https://www.wnyc.org/story/301027-deconstructing-martin-luther-king-jrs-dream/
[121] S.E. Smith, *Dancing in the Street*, p.122

[122] Ibid, p.15

Party used images of Motown and its success to promote its black nationalist 'agendas of economic and political empowerment.'[123] During the early and middle years of the twentieth century, Detroit, and the black capitalism and the 'self-help strategies' that influenced it, would also become the home of some of the most powerful black nationalist agendas and organisations in the United States. As Smith argues, this was no mistake as there was really no place like Motown.[124] The deep intertwining of the economic success and independence of some of the black community through Motown Records, the black philosophies of Malcolm X and Booker T Washington, and the emergence of black nationalist parties such as the Freedom Now Party in Detroit, all show the extensive relationship between the cultural politics, economic independence and the racial fight for freedom.[125]

The story that emerges from these intertwining's, and of Detroit in the mid twentieth century, is how all aspects of the black community, its beliefs and philosophies worked together to empower the black community and create political strength.[126] The story of Motown that

---

[123] Ibid, p.92
[124] Ibid, p.58
[125] Ibid, p.58
[126] Ibid, p.59

has been presented here offers an example of not only what was possible through economic independence but also what could be achieved through following the philosophies presented throughout the black freedom struggle. Motown is ultimately a powerful example of how following black philosophies and empowering the black community can change the course of the future.[127] Not only did Motown advance the economic situation of blacks in Detroit but it also provided hope and inspiration for the black community to stand up against the racism, segregation and discrimination that 'the civil rights movement rallied against.'[128] Motown became the model example for black capitalism and black accomplishment throughout the whole of America; as Boyce states, it was 'a black business in Detroit capitalising on the city's black talent.'[129] Motown's achievements of black economic independence were highly commended by the Detroit branch of the NAACP in 1963. Gordy was highly praised for his efforts 'in opening the field to Negroes' and allowing Detroit's black community to be 'recognised as the centre of the rhythm and blues recording industry'; Gordy also won awards during Small Business Week in Detroit which also shows how

---

[127] Ibid, pp.20, 16
[128] A.K. Boyce, *"What's Going On"*, p.82
[129] A.K. Boyce, *"What's Going On"*, p.49; S. E. Smith, *Dancing in the Street*, p.90

extensive his influence on the community was. [130] Ultimately Motown records was accomplishing what Booker T Washington and Malcolm X had been echoing throughout black communities – economic self-help, economic independence and economic success.[131]

Figure 15 - Berry Gordy receiving an award from Small Business Week

---

[130] A.K. Boyce, *"What's Going On"*, p.66; State University Libraries, *Gordy, Berry Jr., President Motown Records (Small Business Week)* (Online) Available at: https://digital.library.wayne.edu/item/wayne:vmc26608_1
[131] S. E. Smith, *Dancing in the Street*, p.88

'What's Going On?' – Political Recordings and Political Expression

After the success of Motown's release of the Great March to Freedom album in 1963, and Gordy realising the importance of preserving the voices of the black freedom struggle, it was decided the subsidary label Black Forum would be created. The label would preserve many political voices in such a crucial era whilst allowing Motown to distance themselves from any controversial political energies of the time. Black Forum is one of the many subsidiary labels owned by Motown; the recordings of the label consist of eight albums and one single and these recordings hold the most overt political statement of Motown's career.[132] It is noted that Motown founded the Black Forum subsidiary 'as a medium for the presentation of ideas and voices of worldwide struggle of black people to create a new era… [and as] a permanent record of the sound of the struggle.'[133] The eight recordings consist of black political and culutral voices such as Stokely Carmichael, Langston

---

[132] C. E. Sykes, "The Black Forum Label: Motown Joins the Revolution." *ARSC Journal* 46.1 (2015), p.2

[133] S.E. Smith, *Dancing in the Street*, p.17

Hughes, Black Panther Party chairman Elaine Brown, Amiri Baraka, and of course Martin Luther King Jr.[134] The Black Forum allowed Motown to not only engage indirectly with the black freedom struggle but also show that as a black company its awareness was broad and went beyond creating black music.

Figure 16 - Writers of the Revolution album cover

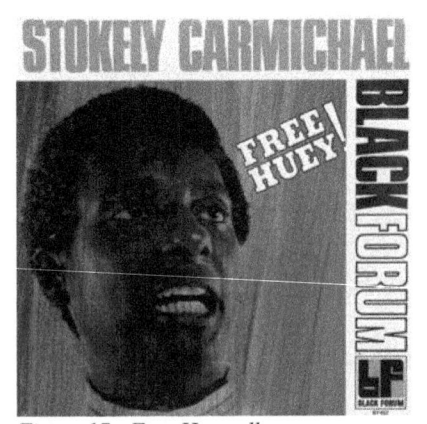

Figure 17 - Free Huey album cover

---

[134] C. E. Sykes, "The Black Forum Label", p.1; S. Carmichael, *Free Huey* (Black Forum, 1970); L. Hughes & M. Danner, *Writers of the Revolution* (Black Forum, 1970)

Gordy understood his role clearly in helping to 'preserve black history and culture.'[135] He also knew that these recordings would be aiding the fight for civil rights as they were 'authentic materials' that could be used in 'schools, colleges and for the homestudy of black history and culture.'[136]

When Gordy first began his Black Forum recordings, they did not provide any economic benefits to the Motown Recording Company, nor were they very popular at the time of recording. However, they show that Motown was politically aware and prepared to aid the black freedom struggle and those influential people within it.[137] They prove, as with Motown's Great March to Freedom album, that Motown was prepared to enter the politics of racial struggle and support its people through preservation, education and media representaiton.

Furthermore, throughout the early to mid sixties Hitsville USA maintained its role of producing black music that would reach the charts, and in many cases reach number one. Its lyrics usually spoke about love, heart break or friendship, but many of its audiences picked up concealed

---

[135] S.E. Smith, *Dancing in the Street*, pp.231, 17
[136] Ibid, p.230
[137] C. E. Sykes, "The Black Forum Label", p.34

messages in Motown's lyrics way before Gordy allowed his artists to produce message music. Many interpreted the sound or lyrics of particular songs as having hidden meanings in relation to the black freedom struggle.[138] Songs like Martha & the Vandellas 'Heatwave', 'Dancing in the Street' and 'Nowhere to Run' captivated audiences into believing the songs had more meanings than simply being about love, dancing and heartbreak, despite not being described explicitly as message music. Others interpreted songs such as Jr Walker & the All Stars 'Shotgun' and Kim Weston and Marvin Gaye's duo 'It Takes Two' as symbols of the 'volatile civil rights struggle'; 'It Takes Two' could be interpreted 'as an endorsement of desegregation', but you could still dance to it as if it represented two lovers.[139]

It wasn't just public listeners who interpreted Motown's hits in this way either. Both Marvin Gaye and Amiri Baraka both interpreted songs, particularly by Martha & the Vandellas, as having political meaning. Amiri Baraka expressed that Martha & the Vandellas music 'provided

---

[138] S.E. Smith, *Dancing in the Street*, p.140
[139] S.E. Smith, *Dancing in the Street*, p.153, C., Werner, *A Change is Gonna Come*, p.27; M. Reeves & The Vandellas, *Heatwave* (Gordy, 1963); M. Reeves & The Vandellas, *Dancing in the Street* (Gordy, 1964); M. Reeves & The Vandellas, *Nowhere to Run* (1965); Jr Walker & The All-Stars, *Shotgun* (Soul, 1965); M. Gaye & K. Weston, *It Takes Two* (Tamla, 1966)

a core of legitimate social feeling, though mainly metaphorical and allegorical for black people.'[140] Marvin Gaye claims that he really thought that Martha & the Vandellas 'came closest to saying something... they captured a spirit that felt political.'[141]

***

The Temptation's 'Cloud 9' was the first song that conveyed essences of message music released by Motown, and many of the Temptations songs were 'overt in their message.'[142] 'Ball of Confusion' expressed the mounting problems, in the late sixties, that were gripping the whole of America – 'people moving out, people moving in. Why? Because of the colour of their skin... Well, the only person talking about love thy brother is the preacher... Segregation, determination, demonstration, integration, aggravation, humiliation, obligation to our nation.'[143] It was Gaye who first felt the need to approach Gordy about recording message music, 'with the world exploding around me, how am I supposed to keep singing love songs?' he explained during the height of

---

[140] B., Ward, *Just My Soul Responding*, p.204
[141] Ibid, p.204
[142] S.E. Smith, *Dancing in the Street*, p.234; A.K. Boyce, *"What's Going On"*, p.77; The Temptations, *Cloud 9* (Gordy, 1969)
[143] A.K. Boyce, *"What's Going On"*, p.77; The Temptations, *Ball of Confusion* (Gordy, 1970)

the civil rights movement and the emergence of the Black Power movement.[144] With the emergence of the Black Power movement, there was a shift in many artists' ideas of what was important to the black community. It was becoming increasingly important to be heard and express views and support for the, what seemed to be, everlasting black struggle for freedom. Marvin Gaye explained that 'suffering and injustice are things which I've always felt deep in my soul, and I wondered what I was doing singing… instead of leading the marchers. I know I had that ability, but that wasn't my role. Years later when Bob Marley came around, I saw that both things were possible. His music caused political change, and that's why he'll occupy a high place in history.'[145]

With the changing political and social climate, Motown released a full message music album by Marvin Gaye called 'Whats Going On?'. The album captured the political and social tensions and problems that were gripping black America at the time - 'trigger happy policing… panic is spreading… God knows where we're heading.'[146] The album broke new ground, and it is considered to be one of Motown's best albums to this

---

[144] S.E. Smith, *Dancing in the Street*, p.170
[145] S.E. Smith, *Dancing in the Street*, p.237
[146] M. Gaye, *Inner City Blues (Make Me Wanna Holler)* (Tamla, 1971)

day, reaching number 6 on the Billboard Hot 200. It proved to Motown and its artists that there was a need for culturally powerful blacks to speak out to America surrouding the issues its community were facing.[147]

---

[147] S.E. Smith, *Dancing in the Street*, p.238

'The Sound of Young America' – The Erosion of Racial Barriers[148]

Figure 18 - The Motown Sound Flyer

Since the Second World War the barriers that separated blacks and whites had begun to break down and music held a place in every culture. Particularly, it created a 'unique...dialogue... between black and white' people.[149] When Berry Gordy created his motto for Motown Records, 'The Sound of Young America', he underestimated the 'social and political implications of his word' - the Motown Sound eventually eroded racial barriers in a country that, in its South 'a white man could murder an African American for brushing up against him.'[150]

What began as aspiring to be 'The Sound of Young America' soon became the sound of the whole of America, and eventually the world; it

---

[148] Detroit Historical Society, *The Motown Sound flyer* (1966) (Online) Available at: https://detroithistorical.pastperfectonline.com/archive/68D0A489-8515-4A9C-BCDE-561117777476
[149] Werner, C., *A Change is Gonna Come*, p.xii
[150] A.K. Boyce, *"What's Going On"*, p.29; S. Wendt, *The Spirit and the Shotgun Armed Resistance and the Struggle for Civil Rights* (Florida, 2010), p.13

was true that Motown songs spoke 'deeply to almost everyone who… heard them'[151] Additionally, Motown gave blacks the chance to have a collective identity and racial pride, but it also allowed whites a chance 'of getting past white.'[152] As Gordy explained 'there were white people around the world whose main connection to black culture had been through our music', and the way Motown entered the lives of white America in a time when many would not allow blacks to enter their neighbourhoods was 'no small feat' in the aiding of the black freedom struggle.[153] Both Motowns aim to reach a crossover audience and the development of the civil rights movement in the sixties go hand in hand, both compliment each other. Changing race relations led to changing public opinion and the emergence of a sophisticated black musical sound added to this.[154]

Many understood the importance of Motown and its artists breaking through to white audiences, and Gordy's success in reaching a biracial audience allowed blacks to enter the homes and lives of whites through

---

[151] Ibid, p.83
[152] Werner, C., *A Change is Gonna Come*, pp.19, 66
[153] A.K. Boyce, *"What's Going On"*, pp.45, 46; B. Gordy, *To Be Loved: the Music, the Magic, the Memories of Motown* (2017), p.17
[154] S.E. Smith, *Dancing in the Street*, p.7

records and radios.[155] It was clear that this new acceptance of the African American race into the homes and lives of white America prophisised the evolving and changing race relations that were to come throughout the sixties.[156]

Firstly, Gordy was extremely focused on the way his artists came across in public light. Teaching etiquette classes and having a 'quality control' department, Motown's unique way of promoting and publicising its artists in a well mannered and sleek way, presented the Motown Sound in a way as not to 'contribute to any racist stereotypes of African Americans.'[157] With more people challenging the core of racism and segregation in America during the sixties it was important that the black community had positive projections to the nation; refined and sophisticated images and TV appearances of Motown artists provided assurance to 'the American public at a time when… racial tensions… loomed.'[158] It can be duly argued that the way Gordy projected his artists, and the songs they sung, allowed them to be accepted into white America; Motown and its artists defied racial stereotypes and proved

---

[155] A.K. Boyce, *"What's Going On"*, pp.45, 46
[156] B., Ward, *Just My Soul Responding*, p.128
[157] S.E. Smith, *Dancing in the Street*, p.121
[158] Ibid, p.135

that black America was not much different than white America. This can be seen in accounts such as that of journalist Dave Marsh who claims when he heard Smokey Robinson singing 'You've Really Got a Hold On Me' it disintegrated the racist premises that he had grown up hearing and believing – 'the depth of feeling in that Miracles record… overthrew the premise of racism, which was that blacks were not as human as we, that they could not feel – much less express their feelings – as deeply as we did.'[159]

Additionally, together, Gordy, Motown's in house band the Funk Brothers, and others created what is known to be the 'Motown Sound'; the sound laid the backing track to the civil rights movement and the early years of the Black Power movement. It created black economic independence, spoke to and inspired many African American youth and it also eroded racial barriers.[160] Out of all the emerging black record labels during the decade, none would reach white audiences as well as Motown.[161] Consequently, many Motown artists observed for themselves the intangible and physical barriers that were being eroded

---

[159] B., Ward, *Just My Soul Responding*, p.232
[160] A.K. Boyce, *"What's Going On"*, pp.34, 64
[161] Ibid, p.161

because of the music they were singing. In many concerts, particularly in the South, there would be, as Ralph Bass noted, 'a rope across the middle of the floor. The blacks on one side, whites on the other, digging how the blacks were dancing and copying them.'[162] As Otis Williams of The Temptations also recalls when touring in South Carolina, he was shocked to see a rope dividing the audience 'angry, we asked, "what the fuck is the rope for?" But we knew the answer. There were far too many scenes like that to recount.'[163] Eventually, these physical barriers would be broken and the metaphorical ones would follow. Bass also notes how when 'the rope would come down. They'd [black and whites] all be dancing together. And you know it was a revolution. Music did it. We did it as much with our music as the civil rights acts and all of the marches, for breaking the race thing down.'[164] Otis Williams also remembers revisiting that same town in South Carolina and the rope was gone, as he explains 'in only a matter of months, some of those barriers fell, at least among the young people.'[165] Other accounts such as Bruce Springsteen recollecting his youth in the sixties explain that 'Motown

---

[162] Ibid, p.130
[163] O. Williams, & P. R. Bashe, *Temptations* (New York, 2017), p.79
[164] B. Ward, *Just My Soul Responding,* p.130
[165] O. Williams, & P. R. Bashe, *Temptations,* p.79

was the only force that could bring détente to the dance floor. When Motown was played, everyone danced together.'[166] Motown knew a song would be a hit when staff would take the unreleased record home and their 'kids could dance to it. White kids.'[167]

The Chronicle commended Gordy for creating 'an international art form that promoted interracial understanding'; it is clear Motown truly helped to erode racial barriers.[168] There was a common music interest among Americas youth and that meant that both blacks and whites could dance together, and this was Motown's primary goal when founded. It cannot, and should not, be forgotten that the Motown sound 'was always Brown'. But ultimatley, the acceptance of the black music Motown was producing, ushered in and supported the acceptance of blacks into the wider American community where they would never have held a comfortable place before.[169]

---

[166] B. Springsteen, *Born to Run* (New York, 2016)
[167] B. Gordy, *To Be Loved*, p.170
[168] S.E. Smith, *Dancing in the Street*, p.144
[169] Ibid, p.167

Our tours made breakthroughs and helped weaken racial barriers. When it came to the music, segregation didn't mean a thing in some of those towns, and if it did, black and white fans would ignore the local customs to attend the shows. To see crowds that were integrated - sometimes for the first time in a community - made me realise that Motown truly was the sound of young America. – Mary Wilson.[170]

Motown and its creation of the 'Sound of Young America' not only provided a backing track and sound track to the sixties in America, but it also the black freedom struggle. It fitted with Kennedy's New Frontier 'which relied on the social commitment of young people' all over America.[171] It provided a common interest and popular culture between both the black and white communities, whilst also proving many racist premises were far from true; Motown was a bridge that white America could use to relate to the black community. The Motown Sound provided 'black cultural expression' that held an immense 'power to promote interracial understanding.'[172]

---

[170] M. Wilson, *Dreamgirl and Supreme Faith: My Life as a Supreme* (New York, 1999), p.125
[171] S.E. Smith, *Dancing in the Street*, p.152
[172] Ibid, p.136

Essentially, by creating the 'Sound of Young America' Motown supported the black freedom struggle without being overtly political, and not steering away from Gordy's goals to reach a crossover audience. By listening to this music, 'the youth of America came together and implemented the civil rights principles of integration and cooperation.'[173] It is easy to argue that the Motown Record Company created a sound that brought together the black and white community through the beats, and dance moves of black America.[174] Motown and its artists witnessed the horrors of racism, segregation and Jim Crow, but they also saw, before their very own eyes, how they were eroding those horrors - as Martha Reeves explains 'the Motown sound was a very big influence in the civil rights movement.'[175]

---

[173] A.K. Boyce, *"What's Going On"*, p.78
[174] Ibid, p.78
[175] M. Reeves, and M. Bego, *Dancing in the Street: Confessions of a Motown Diva* (New York, 1994), p.119

'634-5789 Soulsville, USA': Integration, Opportunity and Stax Fax

There's an old saying

that goes like so,

keep trying

and you'll get where you want to go.

When things get rough

buckle down

don't give up,

you can conquer the world with your original sound.

They knocked at the front door

and couldn't get in,

they heard a sound and went to the back door

thus the sound let them in.

– unattributed poem in a Stax publicity release[176]

---

[176] P. Guralnick, *Sweet Soul Music,* p.97

Figure 19 - Estelle Axton outside Stax

As Peter Guralnick explains, the poem up above comes as close as any of the telling's of Stax's creation and its impact on America.[177] 'They knocked at the front door and couldn't get in, they heard a sound and went to the back door and thus the sound let them in', this particular line acts as a testimony of the initial early rejection from the mainstream of black music and those who sung it.[178] To be black and to want to enter the music industry many had to go through the metaphorical back door, before they could enter the front door of mainstream attention. But Stax records changed this. Stax records would become famous through the voices of Otis Redding, Sam & Dave, Carla Thomas, Rufus Thomas,

---

[177] Ibid, pp.97, 98
[178] Ibid, p.97

Booker T & the MG's, Wilson Pickett and Isaac Hayes.[179] What became known as the Memphis Sound soon became popular throughout America.

Gospel influences were still prominent, just like in Motown. As Booker T Jones of Booker T & the MG's expressed 'The Memphis sound started in a church'. Still, as co-founder Jim Stewart remarked in an interview for *Billboard* magazine 'the sound is hard to describe. It was a heavy black beat. We accent the beat and rhythm in our recordings.'[180] Eventually Stax would counter Motown's 'Hitsville USA'; on the outside of the old movie theatre that was recently converted into the Stax recording studio hung the words Soulsville USA.[181] Additionally as Motown had their very own 'Ain't No Place Like Motown' record, Atlantic through Stax released Wilson Pickett's '634-5789, Soulsville USA', a direct contrast to the Velvelettes 'Ain't No Place Like Motown' in both title and sound.[182] The music coming out

---

[179] R. Gordon, *Respect Yourself*, p.8

[180] B., Ward, *Just My Soul Responding*, p.184; 'Memphis sound: a southern view' *Billboard Magazine*, June 12, 1969

[181] P. Guralnick, *Sweet Soul Music*, p. 97; Photograph available at: A., Lisle, *Soulsville: How It All Began* (2019) Online (Available at: https://memphismagazine.com/features/soulsville-how-it-all-began/ (Accessed: 4/5/21)

[182] The Velvelettes, 'Ain't No Place Like Motown', *A Cellarful Of Motown, Motown* (Album, 2002); Pickett, W., *634-5789 (Soulsville, U.S.A),* (Atlantic, 1966)

of Stax in Memphis can be seen as a more authentic black sound because the music spoke of the struggles and lives of the black community, and was much more relatable to the black community who were listening to it. Listening to the two songs by The Velvelettes and Wilson Pickett, it is easy to understand why Stax can be considered a more authentic black sound through its rhythms and beats, and despite this song not explicitly speaking of Southern black struggles, the echoes of the American South, Jim Crow segregation and scenes like the banks of the Mississippi river resonate in its mood. *The Tennessean Sun* defined the differences between the sounds as Stax displaying 'the Memphis style of soul music, in contrast to… Motown… which is produced so that every particle of sound is planned ahead.'[183]

Although Motown and Stax, simply through their different sounds, highlight the differences of cities in the North and South, nothing highlights the racial splits in society more than the sounds of soul and country music.[184] As Hughes explains, the differences between soul and country music became the 'shorthand for the distance between black and white.'[185] Yet physically those distances could not have been closer in

---

[183] 'Redding's 'Dock' Soars After Tragedy' *The Tennessean Sun,* April 14, 1968
[184] C. L. Hughes, *Country Soul*, p.1
[185] Ibid, p.6

Tennessee, both musically and physically: Nashville became the home of country music and Memphis the home of soul.[186] But the popularity of soul, and the fact that whites in Memphis played a huge part in its production are facts that stand as 'a symbolic testament to the durability of integrationist sentiments.'[187]

The power and influence having white skin held in the American South was 'both stark and subtle.' The South was a strange and harsh place to be if the colour of your skin was not white. It was a place where racism, segregation and plantation mentality had changed little since emancipation. As Werner explains, a white man would not let you shake his hand if you were black, but he would only let a black person cut and wash his hair, and 'black breasts could suckle white babies' but if a black person tried on an item in a store it would be 'rendered unfit for sale to white people.'[188] As Booker T, a Stax artist, remembered, 'when I was growing up, if a report that a white man was shot came into the police station in downtown Memphis, they would launch an investigation. If a black man shot a black man, they would just go out

---
[186] Ibid, p.21
[187] B., Ward, *Just My Soul Responding*, p.218
[188] C. Werner, *A Change is Gonna Come*, p.57

for more coffee...'.

In contrast to Motown, who broke social racial and segregation barriers down, even eventually in the South, Stax in Memphis was the fear of many White Citizens' Council's. They wanted nothing more than to 'do away with this vulgar animalistic nigger' music, which could drive the 'white man…. to the level of the nigger.'[189] But the influence of white men in the creation and success of Stax records would prove to the White Citizens' Council that many had already gotten to that level, and what a good level it was to be at.

Racism was rife in the South and it is no coincidence why the civil rights movement 'consistently avoided Memphis' and stuck to the smaller towns of 'Alabama, Georgia and Mississippi'; even King's advisers were reluctant for him to engage with the Sanitation Workers Strike in Memphis, and ultimately their concerns were confirmed. His decision to participate led King to the balcony of the Lorraine Motel.[190]

Many have investigated the role of Stax in the black freedom struggle by focusing on the company as representing the 'southern dream of freedom' by allowing integration within its studios and on its records to

---

[189] Ibid, p.58
[190] Ibid, p.63

flourish; many speak of an integrationist utopia where the laws of the South were bypassed in a romanticised way.[191] Some, like Hughes, disregard this utopian imagery and show that discrimination and racism were still prominent besides the uniqueness of integration within the studio.[192] But only some have looked at the role Stax played within the Jim Crow South.

It is important not to underemphasise the treatment of blacks in areas which even when the Civil Rights Act was passed in 1964, de facto racism still lingered and little had changed in society.[193] This writing, therefore, is going to explore the aspects of the integration and opportunity that Stax provided in relation to black experience in the South. It will also investigate the importance of the Stax publication *Stax Fax* within the black community – something which has been highly overlooked in the field so far. Running from autumn 1968 to 1970, its twelve issues went on to promote not only Stax's artists and their work, but also problems and challenges that were facing the black community. *Stax Fax* was ultimately a way to 'promote causes important to the black community, all the while championing its talented

---

[191] P. Guralnick, *Sweet Soul Music*; R. Gordon, *Respect Yourself*, p.7
[192] C. L. Hughes, *Country Soul*, p.7
[193] C. Werner, *A Change is Gonna Come*

roster of artists.'[194] Deanie Parker, editor of the magazine, oversaw the magazine in every stage, and understood the need to assert Stax and their artists within the black community.

The black community in Memphis had always been politically assertive prior to the release of *Stax Fax*. It has been understood by scholars such as Elizabeth Gritter that the fact black Memphians had a better and more developed relationship with the Kennedy administration, than the white community, shows the extent of the black community's 'political skill'; the same political skill that can be seen in *Stax Fax*.[195] *Stax Fax* also showed solidarity with the community too – like Motown showing solidarity with the black community in Detroit by recording Kings 'Great March to Freedom' speech.[196] Many of the articles written in the magazines were by influential writers such as journalists who worked for the *Wall Street Journal,* or by members of influential groups

---

[194] Stax Archives, *Stax Fax* (Online) Available at: http://staxarchives.com/staxfax-landing.php

[195] E. Gritter, 'Black Memphians and New Frontiers: The Shelby County Democratic Club, the Kennedy Administration, and the Quest for Black Political Power, 1959-64' in, eds. Goudsouzian, A & McKinney Jr, C. W., *An Unseen Light: Black Struggles for Freedom in Memphis, Tennessee* (Kentucky, 2018), p.189

[196] Stax Archives, *Stax Fax*

such as CORE.[197] Just under sixty percent of the issues contain at least one article surrounding the empowerment of, or the problems faced by, the black community.[198] Just under half of the issues mention black leaders or influential members of the black community such as TV personal or other artists, and issues 6 through 10 hold a substantial amount of socially and politically motivated articles.[199] Therefore, this writing will focus on the political, social, and economically focused articles published in *Stax Fax* and how they relate to wider literature surrounding the black freedom struggle, whilst also exploring the significance of the publication on the black community in Memphis.

---

[197] Stax Archives, Stax Fax Issue 9 (August, 1969) (Online) Available at: http://staxarchives.com/staxfax-book-sf9.php

[198] Stax Archives, *Stax Fax Issue 4, 5, 6, 7, 8, 9, 10* (Online) Available at: http://staxarchives.com/staxfax-landing.php

[199] Stax Archives, *Stax Fax Issue 6, 7, 8, 9, 10* (Online) Available at: http://staxarchives.com/staxfax-landing.php

Growing Green Onions and Planting the Seeds of Opportunity

When Wilson Pickett flew to Memphis, he expressed that he could not believe it, 'I looked out the plane window, and there's these people picking cotton. I said… 'I ain't getting off this plane, take me back North.' Pickett expressed that the echoes of slavery were much too prominent for his liking, and as he had flew down from Detroit it shows instantly the differences between southern culture and the northern one he was used to.[200]

There is no doubt that the Memphis Sound Stax was producing was so different than the sweet sounds of Motown because of the enduring racism its artists and staff experienced.[201] One could never tell with blues, rhythm and blues and soul, how much 'fire came from the Devil and how much came from the Lord.'[202] In 1969 issue 5 of *Stax Fax* explained, the sounds of sixties black America can be described as the 'telling's of the inner feelings of a race that is held in bondage… with a

---

[200] C. Werner, *A Change is Gonna Come*, p.59
[201] Ibid, p.56
[202] Ibid, p.57

fantastic expression of hope for the future.'[203] Additionally, as the *Johnson City Press-Chronicle* stated in 1969 a 'blend of blues, jazz, spirituals and a touch of corn' influenced a sound that became the Memphis sound - a sound that 'cut across ethnic and cultural lines.'[204]

Figure 20 - Green Onions single record sleeve

Green Onions – arguably the most recognisable song to this day produced by Stax – set up Booker T & the MG's fame. Steve Cropper and Duck Dunn, two white men formed Stax's first in house band with black men Booker T and Al Jackson.[205] With Steve Cropper, a white guitar player bringing a country feel and Booker T creating an African

---

[203] Stax Archives, *Stax Fax Issue 5* (March, 1969), (Online) Available at: http://staxarchives.com/staxfax-book-sf5.php

[204] 'The Memphis Sound… A new music discovered for all people discovered' *Johnson City Press-Chronicle,* March 19, 1969

[205] Booker T & The MG's, *Green Onions* (Reissue, Atlantic, 1979); 'Booker T & The MG's: Recording stars have made Memphis soul sound into major musical commodity' *Ebony Magazine*, (1969)

American church feel with the organ it allowed the song to become a merging of the two races, both musically, and physically.[206] The song was a 'fantastic groove' explains Jim Stewart; when the Stax staff heard it 'they came into the control room' and were 'jumping up and down.'[207]

Figure 21 - Cover page of Ebony article

---

[206] R. Gordon, *Respect Yourself*, p.46
[207] Ibid, p.46

Figure 22 - Booker T & the MG's

Ebony magazine published a whole six-page article showcasing the band from its creation in 1961, in their April addition of 1969, describing and highlighting the uniqueness of the Memphis Sound and the interracial aspect of the band.[208] *The Arizona Republic* also credited Stax's unique integrated work setting, describing it as 'one of the most integrated companies in the United States' and that this integration had

---
[208] Ibid

'richened the sound of Stax.'[209] As Booker T explained, 'you don't have white and black working closely together... without developing some kind of family unit. That unit became an example of how the races could escape the plantation mentality... The MG's did love each other.'[210] To many scholars, this integration alone signified the breaking down of racial barriers in the South and, for them, it puts Stax on a pedestal for integrationism and allows the company to be seen as a raceless utopia.[211] Of course integrationism is important in this story, and as issue 2 of *Stax Fax* expresses in 1968, Stax's motto was 'Look what we have done together.'[212]

---

[209] 'Stax Records Define the Memphis Sound' *The Arizona Republic,* June 24, 1969
[210] B. T. Jones, *Time is Tight,* p.159
[211] C. L. Hughes, *Country Soul*; P. Guralnick, *Sweet Soul Music*
[212] Stax Archives, *Stax Fax Issue 2* (1968) (Online) Available at: http://staxarchives.com/staxfax-book-sf2.php

Figure 23 - Integrated Work Force Inside Stax Studio

Stax records define the Memphis sound

BY PETE JOHNSON
Los Angeles Times Service

MEMPHIS — A run-down movie theater in a threadbare black neighborhood is the home of Stax Records, a label whose 40 employes and 10 or 15 major acts are individualistic enough to compete with Nashville, Detroit and San Francisco as a dominant geographic sound in the pop music market.

Memphis, in fact, is challenging Nashville as the voguish place for rootless pop acts to record. Dusty Springfield, White and English, found 'a nice new sound for herself in this nest of rhythm and blues and Elvis Presley, whose first recordings were made in Memphis for Sun Records, returned there to record his last album.

STAX RECORDS is a small label founded in 1957 by Jim Stewart, a former country music fiddle player who was working in the trust department of a bank. Then it was called Satellite Records and its operation was more a hobby for Stewart than a job. "I didn't feel like we were in the record business until 1960," Stewart, now president of Stax, says. "It was sort of an on-again off-again type thing." The turning point came in 1960 with a record called "Gee Whiz" by Carla Thomas, the first national hit for the record company, but Stewart kept his job with the bank until 1964 or 1965.

In this short time, Stax has created and defined the Memphis sound with a string of successful records, some released on the parent label, others on its Volt subsidiary and others issued by Atlantic Records under a production agreement with Stax. Booker T and the MGs, Otis Redding, Sam and Dave, Wilson Pickett, Carla and Rufus Thomas, Eddie Floyd, Johnny Taylor, The Bar Kays and a score of other artists have recorded on the sloping floors of the label's studios (the floors slope because of the building's cinematic past).

IN 1960, when Stewart and company moved in, the building consisted of the theater, a grocery store, a barbershop, a beauty shop, a television repair shop and a restaurant (called 'Slim Jenkins' joint, which became the title of a Booker T and the MGs instrumental record). One by one, they were absorbed by the growth of the label, which maintained a record store in the lobby of the theater to pay its light bills. All has been paneled and green carpeted into a semblance of unity and purpose but the resulting corridors resemble a maze.

What is the Memphis or Stax-Volt sound? Like Detroit's Motown sound, it is characterized by a heavy beat and a distinctive use of horns.

Stax is perhaps one of the most integrated companies in the United States, its perfection lying in the fact that it seems totally unselfconscious. "We were not even aware that we were different from anyone else until a couple of years ago," Stewart muses, "then some people began telling us we were. I don't think of it at all."

THIS OBSERVATION would be less startling if it were made somewhere other than the southwest corner of Tennessee, where a local radio station announces that "three male coloreds" had robbed a liquor store but Stewart's puzzlement is genuine.

The racial mixture has richened the sound of Stax. Stewart has a background as a country musician and country music is just different enough from, but also sufficiently related to, rhythm and blues as a basic American music to produce an interesting hybrid. "I think being a country musician has been an asset, certainly," says Stewart. "We speak of the roots of this business. Country is much the same in the area of roots, it's the real thing, it's down to earth."

Though known primarily as a rhythm and blues label, Stax is expanding into new areas. "By the end of the year we'll have probably 50 employes," Stewart says. "We have about 10 or 15 key acts now on whom we spend a large percentage of our time but we're certainly developing new acts, especially in the progressive rock field. If we're going to be a major factor in the record business, we must develop these areas."

THE LABEL normally releases about 12 singles a month, of which 60 to 70 per cent pay for themselves, according to Stewart. This is a fairly high batting average in the unpredictable pop music market. One index of their growth is their summer release of nearly 30 albums, a record for the company.

Stax was originally affiliated with Atlantic Records, beginning with Carla Thomas' "Gee Whiz." Atlantic provided distribution and promotion for the foundling company until last year, when Warner Bros. bought Atlantic. "For monetary reasons, we could not reach an agreement with Warner Bros.," Stewart says.

Figure 24 - The Arizona Republic, Stax Records Define the Memphis Sound (24/6/1969)

Yet in the Jim Crow South, nothing mattered more to these artists than race relations.[213] If this integration had happened anywhere other than behind the doors of the Capitol Theatre which was Stax's home, it would not have been accepted.[214] As Booker T expresses, 'the emotion was very extreme in the South… it was out of control… growing up black… shows your awareness of your inequality. What you cannot do, you cannot be, how successful you cannot become…. as soon as you are treated as an equal, however, the Sky turns a brighter shade of blue.'[215] Al Bell recalls, when working with Jim Stewart, being 'amazed to sit in the same room with this white guy who had been a country fiddler… we had separate water fountains in Memphis… but to sit in that office with this white man, sharing the same telephone… and being treated like an equal human being – was really a phenomenon.'[216] Not only does Al Bell highlight the relationship of the country genre to white people in his recollection, but also the extent of how unusual the mixing of both races was in the South.

---

[213] C. L. Hughes, *Country Soul*, p.191
[214] Ibid, p.8
[215] R. Gordon, *Respect Yourself*, pp.48, 49; B. T. Jones, *Time is Tight*, p.65
[216] R. Gordon, *Respect Yourself*, pp.7, 8

What was happening in Stax during that time was an affirmation of how black and white could live side by side in harmony, but it was also a shout for freedom in such a harsh American South – as Werner states it was a pledge, 'dismiss me no more, I am a man.'[217] It proved the black community were no less than the white, and both were not as far away from each other as either country and soul or Nashville and Memphis. In Memphis, the black community had long been thought of by whites as lower than even the lowest class of white people, and plantation prejudices were prominent for over one hundred years after emancipation.[218] As earlier blues songs had revealed, blacks were disposable to the white community and a common saying was 'kill a mule, buy another. Kill a nigger, hire another.'[219] Yet Stax 'broke sale records', proving that segregation could only survive through the 'marginalisation of African American labour' - if blacks were treated unequal in every aspect, segregation would persist in the way of whites having more wealth and opportunity.[220] As Al Bell of Stax recognised,

---

[217] R. Gordon, *Respect Yourself*, p.7
[218] R. Gordon, *Respect Yourself*, p.7
[219] Ibid, p.7
[220] Z. F. Robinson, 'After Stax: Race, Sound and Neighbourhood Revitalisation', in, eds. Goudsouzian, A & McKinney Jr, C. W., *An Unseen Light: Black Struggles for Freedom in Memphis, Tennessee* (Kentucky, 2018), p.357

'the way out of this mess is economic empowerment... the money is flowing back to the community.'[221] Stax was the basis of King's dream and other civil rights principles – integration, black capital, changing racial attitudes, the list could go on.

The non-violent civil rights movement arose during the late 1950s, a similar time to when Stax was founded. In the mid-sixties, both were at their prime, like lit beacons for the black community. When King got shot on the balcony of the Lorraine Motel, and when very shortly after his assassination Stax closed its doors forever, it was like a direct assault on the hope that both the movement and Stax had represented to the black community. As Booker T explains, 'because our studio at Stax records was a made over movie theatre, we convened at the Lorraine's dining room' as it 'provided the only suitable location where black and white could congregate without intervention... so it couldn't have been any closer had he [King] been shot at 926 McLemore' (Stax's studio address).[222] The assassination of King during his first and only visit to Memphis could not have dimmed Stax's light any more than it did. As Booker T stated, 'it was a dreadful mockery of the harmonious racial

---

[221] R. Gordon, *Respect Yourself*, p.76
[222] B. T. Jones, *Time is Tight*, p.157; R. Gordon, *Respect Yourself*, p.118

mixing' and it was a mocking of the opportunities Stax provided the black community, much like the opportunities provided by King.[223]

Ultimately though, when Stax was in its prime, as like the civil rights movement, it provided economic empowerment, employment, and opportunity to the black community in the harsh Jim Crow South. As Al Bell retells, once a white grocery store worker suggested that 'Niggers can't do nothing but sing and dance', he got inspired, though offended, and he realised as much of the black community did, 'singing and dancing, you make a lot of money. So, that's not a problem, that's an opportunity.'[224]

---

[223] B. T. Jones, *Time is Tight*, p.157
[224] R. Gordon, *Respect Yourself,* p.76

Stax Fax: 'Keeping Stax On the Coffee Table, When It Wasn't On the Turntable'[225]

Special Stay-in-School LP Features Stax/Volt Artists

MEMPHIS — Stax/Volt artists are featured in a special "Stay-in-School" campaign album, which is being mailed to 4,000 radio stations and deejays throughout the country. The LP includes talks by the artists as well as previously unreleased performances.

The album, which includes Otis Redding, Carla Thomas, San and Dave, Booker T and the MG's, William Bell, the Mar-Keys, and Rufus Thomas, was prepared, written and waxed as a public service by producers under Al Bell, company vice-president.

Vice-President Hubert Humphrey, who wrote the liner notes for the pressing, invited Redding and Miss Thomas to participate with him in a forthcoming program of the Celebrity Showcase for Youth, which stages visits by show business personalities to urban poverty neighborhoods.

Figure 25 - Billboard mentions Stay in School LP

Many campaigns Stax were involved in benefited the African American community, not only in Memphis but throughout America. In 1967, for example, they released a special promo album titled 'Stay in School'; over four thousand copies were circulated 'by the Department of Labour in August.'[226]

Stax understood the influence it held over the black community, and that is why it vowed to stay involved in campaigns that could better life for African Americans, and the community in which they lived.[227] Not only

---

[225] Ibid, p.146
[226] R. Bowman, *Soulsville, USA*, p.124; 'Stax Stay In School LP Part Of Public Service Thing' *Billboard Magazine*, September 9, 1967

[227] R. Bowman, *Soulsville, USA*, p.126

did Stax release promotional albums, they also influenced the community and provided it with education which led to the betterment of the black community in Memphis.

Figure 27 - Let's Save the Children 'The Staple Singers'

Some of Stax artists were part of a children's book collection produced by 'Let's Save the Children, Inc'. These books were sold to public schools nationwide and emphasised the success of Stax artists such as The Staple Singers. The Staple Singers edition was published in 1972, and as other scholars have understood children's books in the Black Power era changed significantly, they no longer focused on integration and living equal to whites; they began to focus on 'black pride and cultural efflorescence.'[228] This can be particularly seen in these books, as they were written in 'soul rhyme' and 'reinforce the artists' positive role within the black community.'[229] For example, in the Staple Singers edition page four reads 'when 'Pop' is not singing, he likes to help others, he gives a helping hand to some young, singing brothers' – emphasising how these artists did more than just sing but they helped the community too.[230]

There is certainly an emphasis on the need for influential black businesses to help the black community in any way they could. Charles

---

[228] N., Batho, 'Black Power Children's Literature: Julius Lester and Black Power', *Journal of American Studies* (2019), p.26

[229] Stax Archives, *Children's Books* (Online) Available at: http://staxarchives.com/books-landing.php

[230] Ibid

Cabbage, a member of 'The Invaders' a prominent civil rights activism group in Memphis, stated that 'people need to control their own communities... black actualisation and community uplift through institutional development' are the 'strategies central to twentieth-century black organising in the United States'. In a way *Stax Fax* is the perfect example of the recognised 'institutional development', he mentions, that could bring about 'black actualisation and community uplift.'[231]

One notable programme Stax conducted was the Stax Association for Everybody's Education (SAFEE), Jim Stewart explained that 'the day centres' Stax created, 'would be for children whose parents cannot afford to pay to send them to preschools or other centres... the trade school would furnish education for students through high school and for those who cannot afford to attend college or university.'[232] Day centres helped women to gain employment in Memphis during this time, many protests focused on the sufficiency of day care centres and that women

---

[231] Smart City Memphis, *The Invaders: A Uniquely Memphis Story* (2016) (Online) Available at: https://www.smartcitymemphis.com/2016/11/the-invaders-a-uniquely-memphis-story/; A. C. Siracusa, 'Nonviolence, Black Power and the Surveillance State in Memphis' War on Poverty' in, eds. Goudsouzian, A & McKinney Jr, C. W., *An Unseen Light: Black Struggles for Freedom in Memphis, Tennessee* (Kentucky, 2018), p.298
[232] R. Gordon, *Respect Yourself*, p.149

could work if there was better day care. Green presents a photograph of a woman protestor, in her book, with a board reading 'we women are willing to work if we get proper child centres.'[233] Poverty was a pressing problem during the sixties and seventies for both Black and white America, with six million people living in absolute poverty.[234] Poverty was a pressing problem during the sixties and seventies for both black and white America, six million people were living in absolute poverty.[235] Adults and children suffered from 'malnutrition, hunger, chronic diarrhoea [and] open running sores', many children both black and white were worse off in the South of America than in third world countries like Kenya.[236] Initiatives like *SAFEE* provided hope for the community in more ways than one; providing children with a free education whilst also providing day care which allowed mothers to gain employment to ease the results of poverty.

Issue 8 of *Stax Fax*, in June 1969, provides a speech spoken by Dr Julian Bond at a huge gathering at a Stax meeting expressing and highlighting

---

[233] Green, Battling the plantation mentality
[234] F. Kornbluh, 'Food as a Civil Right: Hunger, Work and Welfare in the South after the Civil Rights Act' in, *Labour* 12.1-2 (North Carolina, 2015), p. 135
[235] Ibid
[236] J. C. Cobb, 'Somebody Done Nailed Us on the Cross: Federal Farm and Welfare Policy and the Civil Rights Movement in the Mississippi Delta', *Journal of American History* 77.3 (Indiana, 1990), pp, 926, 934

the problems with poverty in the United States at the time. The presence of Julian Bond at Stax, and the speech he did their, echo the notions of the call for Black Power. Working originally as communications director for SNCC and the editor of SNCC's newspaper, Bond had strong beliefs about the problems facing black America. Bond spoke about the hypocrisy of the Vietnam War and the atrocity and extent of problems on home soil - 'American soldiers are still trying to convince the Vietnamese people of the virtues of American democracy' but 'last November... they elected instead, a man, who has yet to demonstrate he has any kind of concern at all for the poor and black... this country began a remarkable war on poverty. But, unlike the war in Vietnam, this war at home was debated and discussed... this war had great difficulty in getting funds... we live in a country which complains a great deal about rising welfare cost, but it... spends, every month, three billion dollars to determine what kind of future fourteen million Vietnamese shall have' (his opposition of the Vietnam war proved to work against him when he decided to 'run for the Georgia state legislature' as they refused to seat him because of his and SNCC's opposition.)[237] The War

---

[237] Duke University Libraries, *Julian Bond* (Online) Available at: https://snccdigital.org/people/julian-bond/

on Poverty in Memphis was a particularly pressing issue, during the sixties Memphis was the 'largest 'pocket' of concentrated poverty in the state of Tennessee', and both civil rights efforts and those to irradicate poverty were very closely tied.[238]

Furthermore, during the late 1960s, SNCC became more accepting of Black Nationalist beliefs and believed less in King's approach of non-violence.[239] These echoes are also present in the transcript of Bond's meeting at Stax as he takes a pro-black stance - 'I cannot say I am pleased with their [white men's] appearance… I am inclined to believe that when the white man was created, Mother Nature was pretty well exhausted.'[240]

***

One of Stax's biggest community programmes can be seen in the release of its monthly publication *Stax Fax*. Although this publication has been highly neglected by scholars, it is important that its impact on the aiding of racial pride and advancement of the black community are analysed.

---

[238] A. C. Siracusa, 'Nonviolence, Black Power and the Surveillance State in Memphis' War on Poverty', p.281
[239] M. Walmsley, 'Tell It Like It Isn't: SNCC and the Media, 1960-1965', *Journal of American Studies 48:1* (2014), p.297
[240] Stax Archives, *Stax Fax Issue 8* (June, 1969) (Online) Available at: http://staxarchives.com/staxfax-book-sf8.php

The magazine was first thought of during an unstable time for Stax as a business; problems with its 'distribution agreement with Atlantic Records' made President Al Bell of the company think quick about new ways to advertise Stax's products, but it was also felt this was a good time to promote Stax's understanding of what were essentially black problems.[241]

Figure 28 - Title of Stax Fax (Issue 7)

Al Bell, publicist and editor Deanie Parker, and Stax, understood the importance of promoting ideas and educating the black community on the problems that were going on in society. As issue 5 explained in 1969 'the average inner city youngster… is generally black as well as culturally and economically deprived' and that the black media and influential businesses such as Stax should use their position to advance the said 'inner city youngsters' by the 'utilisation of techniques and/or

---

[241] Stax Archives, *Stax Fax*

media to enhance communication with and among these youngsters.'[242] From poverty to promoting young Memphians to stay in school, Stax Fax was revolutionary and it went hand in hand with other initiatives happening in Memphis at the time. In the early months of 1968, a programme called the *Neighbourhood Organising Project* began, and ultimately it's objectives were very similar to those of *Stax Fax*.[243] It focused on Black history, 'black pride and black politics'.[244] The *Tri-State Defender* pushed for support of the programme by writing that the objectives were to develop job opportunities, 'increasing self-awareness...' and organise 'neighbourhood improving projects.'[245] In a way it could be argued that a cultural revolution was happening in Memphis. Initiatives were beginning that focused on culture and the community. They not only worked on advancing Memphian society, but to positively impact the lives of those who had always been marginalised and penalised; 'you must have a cultural revolution before [anything else]... the cultural revolution gives identity, purpose and direction.'[246]

---

[242] Stax Archives, *Stax Fax Issue 5* (March, 1969)
[243] BP in the bluff city, p.83
[244] Bp In the BC, p.102
[245] BP in the BC, p.102
[246] Bp in the Bluff city, p.106

There was certainly an emphasis on the need for influential Black businesses to help the Black community in any way they could. Charles Cabbage, a member of 'The Invaders' a Black Power group in Memphis, stated that 'people need to control their own communities... Black actualisation and community uplift through institutional development' are the 'strategies central to twentieth-century Black organising in the United States'. In a way Stax's publication *Stax Fax* is the perfect example of the recognised 'institutional development' he mentioned, which would bring about 'Black actualisation and community uplift.'[247]

Overtime, the publication begins to become longer and look more professional. The first issue is a front cover presenting an executive's message, a double page spread inside surrounding 'Top Records of the Month' and mentions the progress of Stax's artists, the back cover presents an 'Artist of the Month' page.[248] The pictures are black and white, and the layout is simple – a plain blue and white background to

---

[247] Smart City Memphis, *The Invaders: A Uniquely Memphis Story* (2016) (Online) Available at: https://www.smartcitymemphis.com/2016/11/the-invaders-a-uniquely-memphis-story/; A. C. Siracusa, 'Nonviolence, Black Power and the Surveillance State in Memphis' War on Poverty' in, eds. Goudsouzian, A & McKinney Jr, C. W., *An Unseen Light: Black Struggles for Freedom in Memphis, Tennessee* (Kentucky, 2018), p.298
[248] Stax Archives, *Stax Fax Issue 1* (1968) (Online) Available at: http://staxarchives.com/staxfax-book-sf1.php

each page. However, as the issues begin to grow their layout and front covers begin to change with each issue. One of the last issues, issue 10, consists of 40 pages and contains more politically and socially motivated articles. The magazine was 'directed toward both industry personnel and... popular audience.'[249] There is a consistent pattern that as *Stax Fax* continued to be produced it looked more professional, became more politically and socially aware, and got longer. This may have been because the popularity of the publication increased or simply because the audience grew wider than those just interested in Stax's music. This is extremely positive considering Deanie remembers receiving hate mail when the magazine first became politically aware – 'people didn't want us mailing this "communist propaganda" to their homes. It's black, that makes it communist.'[250]

---

[249] R. Gordon, *Respect Yourself*, p.146
[250] R. Bowman, *Soulsville, USA*, p.160

In some issues there was also promotion to get radio announcers and other influential black businesses to read *Stax Fax* in an effort to keep the black community not only in touch with its youth but also synced with each other – 'black radio announcers should use as much time as possible trying to inspire in young people a sense of pride and self-identity.'[251]

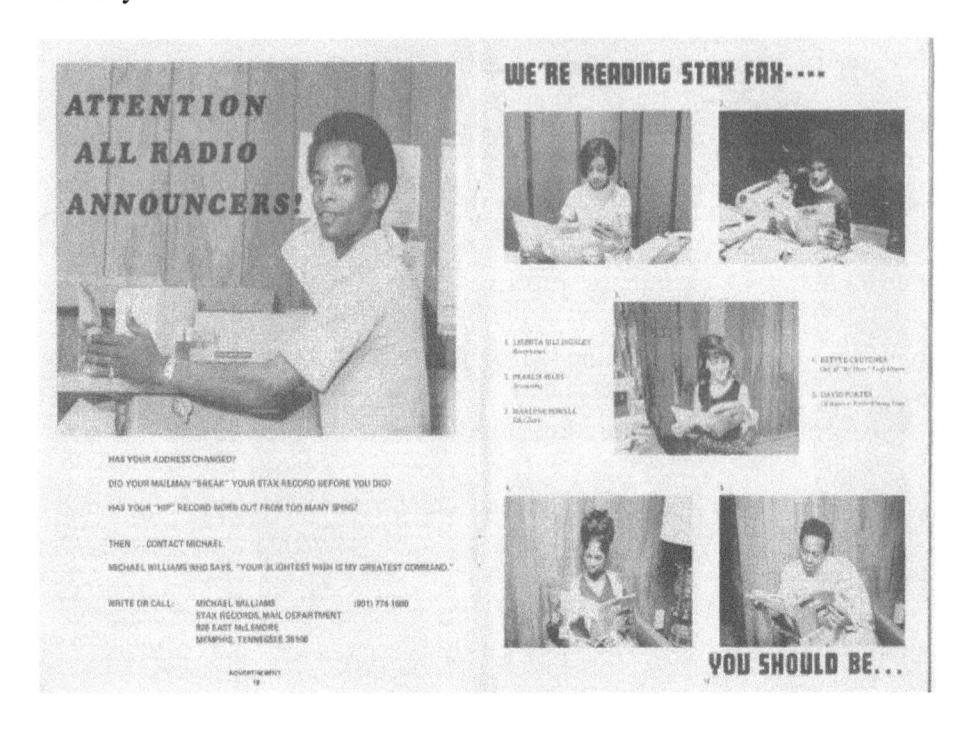

Figure 29 - 'Attention All Radio Announcers' Stax Fax Issue 9 (1969)

---

[251] Stax Archives, *Stax Fax Issue 9* (August, 1969); Stax Archives, *Stax Fax Issue 4* (February, 1969) (Online Available at: http://staxarchives.com/staxfax-book-sf4.php

Figure 30 - Stax Fax for the 'Know' generation (Issue 10)

Stax Fax also helped the 'inner city youngster' in Memphis more directly. As Deanie Parker acknowledges, the release of *Stax Fax* had a huge impact on the community. It gave the mostly disadvantaged teenagers somewhere to 'direct their attention to something positive… we created jobs… here in the community just to get this mailing out'. As Bowman explains when an issue of *Stax Fax* was ready to be mailed out, 'the high school kids who made up the Stax… fan club would come in' and help to box and pack the issue.[252]

This was not the only thing *Stax Fax* did for the community. It educated and made it aware through the abundance of politically, socially and economically motivated articles the magazine contained, particularly towards the black youth of Memphis. These publications can be seen to be more than an acknowledgement to the problems of black America, and more of an attempt to educate the black community and potentially positively impact some of these problems. As issue 4 stated in 1969, Stax knew how important the youth were to the changing of the future – 'our hope for tomorrow lies in young America.'[253] It is no wonder that by issue 10 the appeal of reading the magazine can be seen, as the publication was being described as 'for the "Know" generation'.[254]

Stax Fax was used to educate the community, particularly its youth, about the benefits of doing well in school and why they should stay in school. In 1969 issue 5, a double page spread entitled 'Anything for an A' written by a journalist from the *Wall Street Journal*, educated about the dangers of cheating on papers and exams in college. The article

---

[252] R. Bowman, *Soulsville, USA*, p.160; Stax Archives, Stax Fax Issue 7 (May, 1969) (Online) Available at: http://staxarchives.com/staxfax-book-sf7.php
[253] Stax Archives, *Stax Fax Issue 4* (February, 1969)
[254] Stax Archives, *Stax Fax Issue 10* (September, 1969) (Online) Available at: http://staxarchives.com/staxfax-book-sf10.php

opens up mentioning how a college student quit his respectable job to complete exams and assignments for other students, as by taking 'five exams... [he] pocketed $180.'[255] The article goes on to express how cheating is bad and the punishments involved, concluding that the only way to stop students cheating is 'if the student body at large, and their own circle of friends in particular, disapprove.'[256] The article not only expresses morally important things in its text but the way in which it is laid out allows for a simple read for students of any age.

Figure 31 - 'Stay in School' (Issue 10)

---

[255] Stax Archives, *Stax Fax Issue 5* (March, 1969)
[256] Ibid

125

Issue 10 (September, 1969) of *Stax Fax* hosted an eye-catching page surrounding one of its leading groups at the time. Entitled 'Stay in School with the Bar-Kays', the page presents two images of the group – one outside a bus, and one of them inside. It reads 'The Bar-Kays Are On The Move – Busting across the nation promoting their latest' song, they 'are ready for weekend engagements and a smooth ride home for their school activities during the week.'[257] It was a simple message, but to the youth that read these articles it provided motivational words. If the Bar-Kays, one of Stax's most influential bands of 1969, were going to school and completing school activities, it would provide a grounded influential voice in the lives of the black community's youth in Memphis around the importance of staying in school. Especially as throughout the twentieth century social scientists found that the black community often associated school with failure, and rarely looked at school in a way to gain success.[258] (This particularly resonates to when schools were desegregated, as Fairclough explains in segregated schools Black teachers understood Black pupils and the community in which

---

[257] Stax Archives, *Stax Fax Issue 10* (September, 1969)

[258] A. Fairclough, 'The Costs of Brown: Black Teachers and School Integration', *Journal of American History* 91.1 (2004), p.46

they lived; something which white teachers could not and did not want to do).[259] They could relate to the words written in these publications more than they could relate to Dr King – a preacher's son with a well sustained college education. Stax knew how important it was for the black community to get a good education, as Al Bell explained, 'the way out of this mess is economic empowerment', and education is one of the most important things that could lead to 'economic empowerment' in the black community.[260]

Stax also understood that some of the most pressing topics for the youth of Memphis, and the black community, were not widely spoken about at school. It, therefore, used *Stax Fax* to speak about these topics in more detail.

Issue 7 (May, 1969) of *Stax Fax* directly challenged the emerging thoughts surrounding sex education in American schools. It explains that 'myriad groups have sprung up across the country to denounce sex education as immoral, subversive, communist-inspired, pornographic and psychologically damaging to the young.'[261] Not only does this

---

[259] Ibid, p.44
[260] R. Gordon, *Respect Yourself*, p.76
[261] Stax Archives, *Stax Fax Issue 7* (May, 1969)

article allow Stax to be seen as socially and politically aware, but it also shows they were not afraid to hide it. As the article explains, sex was a taboo subject for many, but Stax understood the need for good sex education for the youth in Memphis as it would help in reducing teenage pregnancy and educate the youth about the basics of reproduction, puberty and the risks surrounding sex.

Articles such as that in issue 10 titled 'Abortion Counsellors', educates and expresses why there was an ongoing fight for women's rights to have an optional abortion. On page 35 the article goes on to say 'those seeking to relax or abolish abortion laws are heartened by two recent legal decisions. New Jersey's supreme court has declared that abortions may be legal in the state if performed by a doctor.'[262] One must keep in mind that abortion was not legalised until 1973 with the *Roe v Wade* case, so Stax was really making an assertion of their political and social awareness, and potentially controversial opinion through this article being published in 1969.[263] The article helps educate the community about abortion, and both the approving and disapproving sides of the argument. It also shows how politically aware Stax was and how they

---

[262] Stax Archives, *Stax Fax Issue 10* (September, 1969)
[263] BBC, *Roe v Wade: What is the US Supreme Court Ruling on Abortion?* (2020) (Online) Available at: https://www.bbc.co.uk/news/world-us-canada-54513499

knew it was important to show they were more than a musical commodity. This, again, would have influenced the community in Memphis by allowing the understanding that these were on going issues that needed attention, and that the community should be more involved and interested in them. It kept people politically aware and offered alternating opinions of topics that would have been of great debate at the time.

Issue 10 also contained an article entitled 'Replacing "The Pill"'. The article goes on to explain the differences between the contraceptive pill and the morning after pill, new research that was ongoing to find a better replacement to the pill and explains how contraception works throughout the article.[264] These were pressing issues that the community and public needed to hear about and be more educated about. *Stax Fax* shows that Stax understood how influential its voice in the community was, and knew how popular its *Stax Fax* publication was, so used this to the advantage of the community. The youth in Memphis, and those who were fans of Stax, were more likely to pick up a copy of *Stax Fax* than they were a mainstream newspaper, considering Stax's influence in Memphis. Stax made a conscious choice to involve such articles

---

[264] Ibid

surrounding controversial and taboo topics such as sex education and abortion.

In April, 1969, in issue 6 of *Stax Fax* there is a double page spread, written by SCOPE, entitled 'How Much Racism is Based on Sex?' It goes on to explain 'three men were found dead... after three white policemen were heard saying to two white prostitutes who knew the three black men, 'what the ---- do you want them for? Aren't we good enough?' This article not only highlights extents of police brutality but also educates about what many scholars have since spoken about surrounding manhood, masculinity, and racism – the fact that white men used women and sex to control and suppress the black man even further than economic, political, and social ways. [265] 'Out of bitterness, jealousy or just mischievous fun a white man or woman could have any black man killed just by pointing a finger at him. It happened many times in the South. A black man would be hung by his wrists from a tree and a public-spirited citizen would cut his genitals off'; torture had always played a big part within lynching, including castration and burning alive

---

[265] Stax Archives, *Stax Fax Issue 6* (April, 1969) (Online) Available at: http://staxarchives.com/staxfax-book-sf6.php; S. Wendt, *The Spirit and the Shotgun*, p.10

- as the National Police Gazette headlined in 1886, nearly one hundred years before this, 'Another Coon to Roast.'[266] Lynching had always been present in the American South and many used sexual fears as a justification for mob violence against African Americans; it became 'the recognised method of re-enslaving blacks.'[267] As Wendt explains, segregationist violence was used to initiate and maintain southern manhood. The fact that these men were being humiliated by having their genitals removed proves how much racism revolved around sex and sexuality, especially as the *Stax Fax* article goes on to explain '"the whites" fear that the black man yearns to rape white women isn't borne out by facts.'[268]

For many years, Southern Democrats had spread and set a light fear of black lust that was far from the truth, simply because they wanted blacks to be seen as less than human and unsuitable for citizenship.[269] As Freedman accounts, Southern Democrats understood that 'political equality breeds ambition for social equality' - something segregationists did not want. Prejudice against black and white relationships lasted well

---

[266] Stax Archives, *Stax Fax Issue 6* (April, 1969); E. B. Freedman, *Redefining Rape: Sexual Violence in the Era of Suffrage and Segregation* (Massachusetts, 2013), p.102
[267] E. B. Freedman, *Redefining Rape,* pp.96, 89
[268] S. Wendt, *The Spirit and the Shotgun,* p.10
[269] E. B. Freedman, *Redefining Rape,* p.91

into the twentieth century, and the way black men were treated for these relations was a disgrace. It was not until 1967 that the Supreme Court established interracial marriage as legal, and Stax, writing two years after this ruling, clearly understood that this was still a pressing issue and a persisting fear in the Southern black community.[270] It was important that the black community knew the wider context of the racism projected on to them because that is the only way change could happen, especially in the South where despite the passing of the Civil Rights Act in 1964, little changed. It was important for the black community to understand why they were being targeted in interracial relationships, segregationist fears and how, therefore, things could change.

---

[270] Tennessee State Government, *Miscegenation* (Online) Available at: https://sharetngov.tnsosfiles.com/tsla/exhibits/blackhistory/pdfs/Miscegenation%20laws.pdf

Figure 32 - Stax Fax Cover with a picture of Dr King

Other *Stax Fax's* talk about racism, Dr King, slavery, and King's assassination. Issue 5 (1969) released an article entitled 'The Urban League' which emphasises that the time in which the article was written was a huge turning point in American history – 'this community of ours and this nation are at one of the great turning points in history.'[271] It talks about the injustices of slavery - 'the slave was beaten and starved into submission in a manner which castrated him psychologically' - and then goes on to mention what are defined as the King years as being recognised by 'the dramatic way in which his marchers forced the nation to see its own ugliness.'[272] This article is influential in expressing the struggles of the black community and educating about them, it is a short 'history of race relations'.[273] It could be argued Stax being a black business in the South owed it to the black freedom struggle to show its awareness of black struggle and the ongoing fight for civil rights, and they did this very well in this article. 'Let this statement take nothing from the memory of our beloved Martin,' the article goes on to say. Even the use of the word 'our' makes the article personable to those in the black community who read it. 'He was the greatest American of the first ¾ of the 20th century. But with all of this greatness, the stubbornness of the American cultural machinery still moved only

---

[271] Stax Archives, *Stax Fax Issue 5* (March, 1969)
[272] Ibid
[273] Ibid

unwillingly, at a snail's pace' in the acceptance of equal and civil rights.[274]

It is quite prominent throughout reading the issues of *Stax Fax* that more focus is placed upon King and his peaceful movement than that of the Black Power movement which was emerging at the time. This could be because Stax did not want to be associated with the misunderstandings surrounding the call for Black Power as a violent shout for black supremacy, which was a false interpretation presented by the white media; stations like NBC admitted that 'what was sexy – and got on the news – was black aggression.'[275] Whatever the reason, Dr King often appears in different issues of *Stax Fax*.

What is particularly interesting is how Stax honours him after his assassination. Firstly, in one edition of *Stax Fax* they produced a calander of events in the years 1968-69 surrounding the assasination of King, James Earl Ray and the sentencing of him. It helps to make clear to the black community what had happened surrounding the case since

---

[274] Ibid
[275] S., Tuck, *We Ain't What We Ought To Be,* p.330

the day of the assassination, which may have been helpful in officialising facts and allowing the community to read a trusted account.

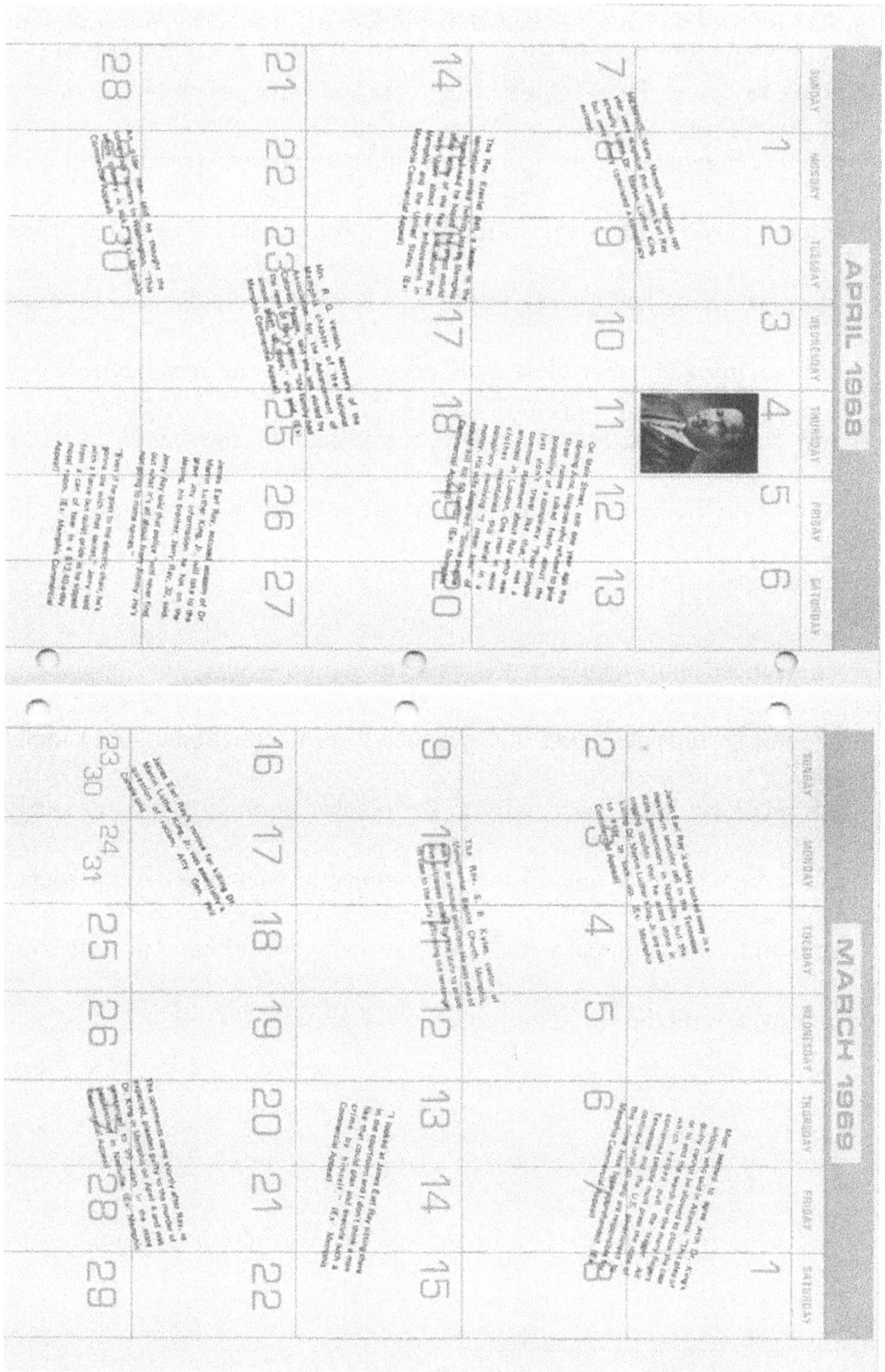

Figure 33 - Comparative Calendar Issue 6

Stax focuses on King's legacy that will live on in African Americans for years to come. They praise his efforts and have an emphasis on the positive things that came from King, his life and campaigns. Writing in Issue 6 (1969), 'Dr King, in the flesh, has gone but his spirit will not die… Dr. King had a large vision of what was attainable and possible through militant non-violence and proved right for he became the leader and symbol of the most effective and influenital movement to affect American life since Abraham Lincoln effixed his signature to the Emancipation Proclomation.'[276]

From these short analyses it is clear to see how Stax went above and beyond its musical talent and purpose to project economic and racial advancement, and opportunity to the black community. It consciously chose to supply its fans in the community of Memphis with a social, economic and political education that many would have not received otherwise, and the community were very grateful for this.

---

[276] Stax Archives, *Stax Fax Issue 6* (April, 1969)

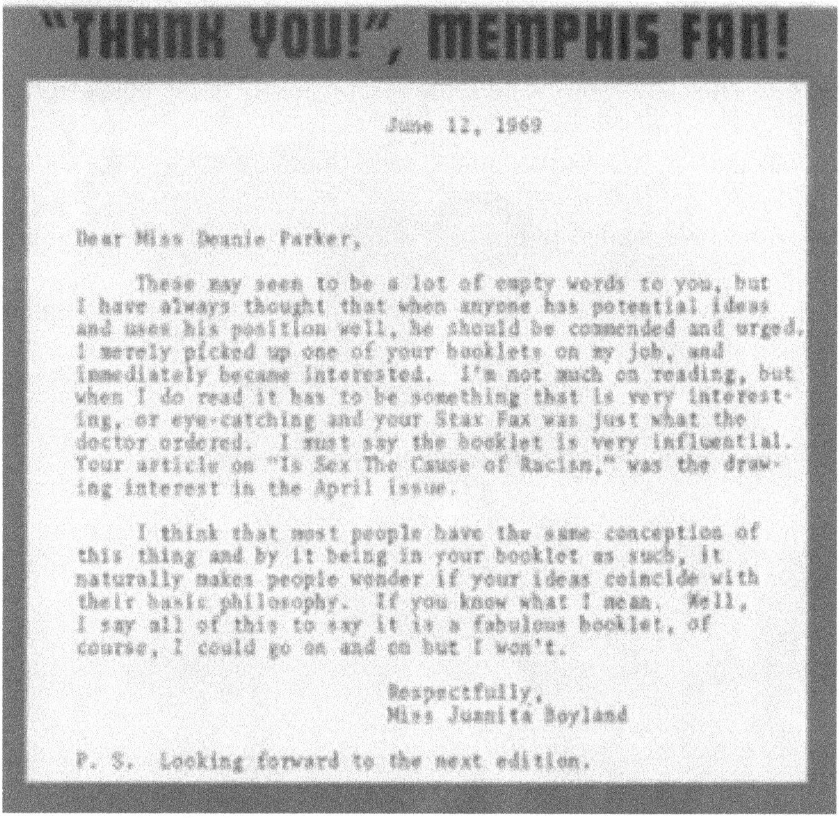

"THANK YOU!", MEMPHIS FAN!

June 12, 1969

Dear Miss Deanie Parker,

These may seem to be a lot of empty words to you, but I have always thought that when anyone has potential ideas and uses his position well, he should be commended and urged. I merely picked up one of your booklets on my job, and immediately became interested. I'm not much on reading, but when I do read it has to be something that is very interesting, or eye-catching and your Stax Fax was just what the doctor ordered. I must say the booklet is very influential. Your article on "Is Sex The Cause of Racism," was the drawing interest in the April issue.

I think that most people have the same conception of this thing and by it being in your booklet as such, it naturally makes people wonder if your ideas coincide with their basic philosophy. If you know what I mean. Well, I say all of this to say it is a fabulous booklet, of course, I could go on and on but I won't.

Respectfully,
Miss Juanita Boyland

P. S. Looking forward to the next edition.

Figure 34 - Thank you message to Stax Fax editor Deanie Parker

The late sixties marked the end of the King era, and race relations, education, politics and economics were greatly changing. These publications known as *Stax Fax* provided a bridge between music, politics, and the community in Memphis. It educated, informed and influenced the community whilst also providing interesting articles on its own business and musical relations and artists.

Overall, *Stax Fax* provides proof, as did Motown, that black businesses and their influence to be able to assert, educate and show solidarity with the black community was greatly influential to the black freedom struggle. The community held more responsibility in the black fight for freedom than is widely recognised, and therefore stories like this one need to be investigated to not only show the power of the community but also prove that it was influential. Ultimately, as Gordon explains, *Stax Fax* kept Stax 'on the coffee table, when it wasn't on the turntable', but it was certainly more than a business promotion.[277]

---

[277] R. Gordon, *Respect Yourself*, p.146

Conclusion: Black is Beautiful

In retellings of the black freedom struggle, and black history, the importance of black music during the twentieth century is often seen as unworthy of scholars' research and time.[278] Being pushed aside, black music's significance to the black and white community during the twentieth century has been neglected in the history of America, the black freedom struggle, and all those countries histories that contain black struggle and hardship. But, it is an important story.

Rhythm and Blues and Soul are the perfect genres to sum up the decades of struggle that many, both black and white, faced during the mid-twentieth century. The sounds echo the voices of the many West Africans who were exposed to 'the nightmare realities of slavery', and they highlight the refusal of the black race to submit and 'simplify [the] reality' they have faced throughout history.[279]

As Ward explains, the story behind music in the twentieth century surrounding the black freedom struggle is one that goes beyond the courtrooms hosting the NAACP, it goes beyond Jim Crow, beyond segregationist violence and seeps into every aspect of what the black freedom movement fought for and changed.[280] It is a history from below

---

[278] B. Ward, *Just My Soul Responding*, p.124
[279] C. Werner, *A Change is Gonna Come*, p.xiii
[280] B. Ward, *Just My Soul Responding*, p.125

that proves community action, motivation and mobilisation were at the heart of the success of the black freedom movement. More often than not the voices and images of King, Malcolm X and others wash away the true roots of the movement and the focus on figureheads leads to the misunderstanding of, and in some cases not discovering, the 'deepest sources of the movements energy.'[281]

The black freedom struggle shared not only the same protest culture such as sit-ins, marches and freedom songs, but it began to share the same popular culture.[282] It is only possible to understand the significance of black music, not only just soul and rhythm and blues, by placing it within the historical context of a race that has endured endless suffering, and that still suffers today.

By focusing on the two case studies of Motown and Stax, this writing has highlighted some of the many roles of music, and its recording studios, in the black freedom struggle of the twentieth century. It has proved that community relations held a unique and significant role in the black freedom struggle; that community empowerment and solidarity, and the working together of two races proves to be a solution

---

[281] C. Werner, *A Change is Gonna Come*, p.4
[282] S., Tuck, *We Ain't What We Ought To Be*, p.289

to hatred and bigotry. That music gave hope, identity, and common ground in a time where those things were far and few between.

Through the circumstances in Detroit and the development of its vast music scene, Motown contributed to solidifying in history the accomplishments of many African Americans in a time that is often associated only with struggle.[283] By focusing on Motown, this writing has proved how black businesses, black media and the black community can all work hand in hand to fight for change.

A focus on Motown's spoken word recording 'The Great March to Freedom' album – in which Motown recorded King's first rendition of his 'I have a dream' speech – has also shown how Motown preserved history for generations to come and supported the black community in a way that was overtly political for the company at the time.[284] By looking at the Great March in more detail it has shown how black business and black media can support the black community and show solidarity with it. The Great March to Freedom proved the collective and political power of uniting the black community, and how asserting them in an organised fashion could show that the demands of the black

---

[283] S. E. Smith, *Dancing in the Street*, p.16
[284] M. L. King, *The Great March to Freedom* (Gordy, 1963)

freedom struggle were serious and important.

By adding to the analysis of Motown's political recordings by examining Motown's Black Forum label and Gordy's decision to record message music, this writing has also argued that those who make music in times of political and social struggle are powerful voices for community, society and provide a voice in times of need. Artists were not politicians or revolutionary leaders, but they held powerful positions in society; they understood that their voices were influential, yet politically neutral, and used this to the advantage of the community. Overall, Motown's recordings held political and social significance whilst also showing solidarity with the black community in the times when it needed it the most.

By showing Motown as an example of black capitalism, this writing has proved how black nationalist beliefs of economic and community empowerment can not only benefit, but also enhance the black community and the opportunities provided to it in a racist society. It proves that black nationalist belief was focused upon enhancing the black community, allowing it to stand alone from white support or influence. Ultimately, this writing has shown that economic independence can uplift a community enough to allow it to assert itself in the sight of struggle.

Motown and the sound it created provided one of the most influential aspects to the changing of race relations in sixties America. Creating a sound that was black, yet sophisticated, allowed the rethinking of racist stereotypes of the time such as 'blacks were not as human as [whites]... that they could not feel – much less express their feelings – as deeply' as white people.[285] It allowed the African American community to enter the homes of white America in a way that was unlike anything before and it was a chance for the white community to test the societal norms and prejiduces of the time. With the sound being much loved by both white and black America, it allowed the races to come together with a mutual interest, passion and culture.

Sixty years after its prime, the Motown Sound creates the nostalgia that blurs the history of black America. But it also shows how, if given the chance, black business, the black race, and the black community can change the world in which they live and rewrite their history. As Boyce states, Motown 'provided hope and heroes' that 'inspired people of all races to fight against the race segregation and discrimination that the

---

[285] Ward, B., *Just My Soul Responding* (London, 1998), p.232

civil rights movement rallied against.'[286] Motown is a testament that African Americans 'fought for freedom in culture as well as politics.'[287]

Stax, in many ways is both similar and different to Motown. Placed in the heart of the South in Memphis, Tennessee racism was prominent, and the societal situation was much different to that of Detroit, Michigan in the North. Being described as an integrationist utopia, where the laws and tradition of the South did not exist, Stax was the home of what would have been uncommon race mixing and, like Motown, it created opportunity for a race that was marginalised. Booker T & the MG's are the perfect example of how black and whites can work together successfully, and they prove that understanding and acceptance go a long way in changing the norms and traditions of a place that was so race focused.

The opportunity Stax provided the African American community in Memphis was also immense, from stardom to simply equal working opportunities and equal respect - Stax was an entity of hope and courage for the Southern black community. It provided a unique work environment that proved segregation would no longer function once

---

[286] A.K. Boyce, *"What's Going On"*, p.82
[287] S., Tuck, *We Ain't What We Ought To Be*, p.306

blacks had equal status, employment opportunity and economic power. To those working within Stax it proved that the two races were not as far apart as white segregationists would like to portray them - it proved that black and whites were the same and should be equal. *Stax Fax* has been of great focus in this writing, and never has it been the centre of focus and attention in scholarship before. *Stax Fax* places the black community at the heart of Stax's interests and consciously producing politically, economically and socially motivated media helped to educate youth on topics which were not openly spoken about in many situations, such as in school. *Stax Fax* placed Stax at the heart of the community and proved that the education and level of awareness of a community is key to its advancement. By discussing important topics, it proves that Stax was more than a musical entity and understood the real-life black struggle. It also emphasises Stax's role in the community, in a non-civil rights focused way, during the late 1960s which is something that has not been detailed so far; it proves that Stax provided opportunity not only through its musical recordings but also through initiatives such as *Stax Fax* and SAFEE. Overall, this writing has shown what happens when black businesses create a black product that speaks to the community. It has shown how black nationalist philosophies can aid not only economic empowerment but also community empowerment. It has shown that acceptance by some in the South was a crucial way to upheave the segregationist violence, and opinion, that was so prominent there. It has shown how small initiatives such as a monthly magazine can change community relations, community education and community hope. But mostly, overall, it has also proven how when the black community work together, it can change itself and its history forever.

***

Black music and its historical context have created a 'mass black consciousness generated by an evolving black freedom struggle' that is ever so prominent today.[288] It was, and is, through a shared popular culture surrounding music that the black community shared a collective identity.[289] Black music, whether it be soul, R&B, reggae or hip-hop, has always been a symbol of power, strength and community for as long as the black race has suffered, and it will continue to be so until the black race suffer no longer.[290]

---

[288] B. Ward, *Just My Soul Responding*, p.184
[289] Ibid, p.206
[290] M. Ellison, *Lyrical Protest,*, p.145

During the decades of King's non-violent movement, the years following his assassination, and during the call for Black Power and racial pride 'many harboured real hopes that the racial nightmare' that has existed in America, and throughout the world, for many years was finally going to end. But as Werner states - 'it didn't. It still hasn't.'[291] The irony, misunderstandings and mis-memories embedded into mainstream teachings of the civil rights and Black Power movements have led to the education of one of the most important revolutions in history to 'become as much a problem as an inspiration for those seeking' to further erode the injustices faced in the world today.[292] And that is why the musical history of this movement is so important to provide the story of collective identity, inspiration and community uprising that is all needed to support the fight for freedom that is still everlasting.

Music is still a powerful way to project messages to the world, to support movements like Black Lives Matter and, still, as then, project the real-life black experience. Artists such as Nas, Damian Marley, Protoje, Kabaka Pyramid, Bruce Springsteen, Dave and Chronixx still

---

[291] C. Werner, *A Change is Gonna Come*, p.4
[292] Ibid

prove the power of music in relation to the ongoing black freedom struggle. In 2001, Bruce Springsteen sang out '41 shots… is it a gun, is it a knife, is it a wallet, this is your life, it ain't no secret… you can get killed just for living in your American skin'.[293] The song projects the story of Amadou Diallo, a Guinea immigrant who was shot 41 times by New York City Police whilst he was reaching for his wallet.[294] Springsteen highlighted the on-going police brutality towards non-whites in America, something which was also highlighted with the death of George Floyd in 2020. Additionally, as Jamaican artist Chronixx sings, 'most time we hear about black, we hear about black magic and black witches, blacklist, black book, black market, black Friday where you spend half your black riches…they never told us black is beautiful.'[295] These lyrics amplify the realities of being black in the modern world and show that despite the King and Black Power years being over, the black freedom struggle is still very much prominent. Music's role in the black fight for freedom should not be forgotten,

---

[293] B. Springsteen, *American Skin (41 Shots)*, (Columbia, 2001)
[294] J. Fritsch, *The Diallo Verdict: The Overview; 4 Officers In Diallo Shooting Are Acquitted Of All Charges (2000) (Online) Available at:* https://www.nytimes.com/2000/02/26/nyregion/diallo-verdict-overview-4-officers-diallo-shooting-are-acquitted-all-charges.html
[295] Chronixx, *Black is Beautiful (Chronology)*, (Soul Circle Music/Virgin EMI, 2017)

particularly as music holds such an important place in the black community. From freedom songs to message music, from community involvement to nationwide publicity, black music, its creators and producers prove that politics creates music, and music expresses politics. Music will be the everlasting testimony to the struggles the black race face daily, and it is a testimony that will last as long as they struggle.

My only hope is that this writing has appropriately portrayed my passion of rhythm and blues and soul music, my passion for the history of a race that has always been marginalised and my understanding of the importance and need, as a historian, to bring up the voices of those people in the past who would have not had been able to assert their voice in the time in which they lived. To show the civil rights movement was more than just 'Rosa sat down, Martin stood up, and the white kids came down and saved the day.' To allow the understanding that the black race and community is more than how it is often represented in history - 'an eternal victim who suffers beautifully.'[296]

---

[296] The Civil Rights Movement: Grass Roots Perspectives, *Description* (2021) (Online) Available at: https://sites.duke.edu/dukecrmsummerinstitute/summer-institute/; E. P. Morgan, 'The Good, the Bad, and the Forgotten Media Culture and Public Memory of the Civil Rights Movement, in *The Civil Rights Movement in American Memory* ed. C. R. Romano & L. Raiford (Georgia, Atlanta, 1992), p.161

My only regret, as with Werner, is that I will not be able to express or show my full passion for the music and how it has spoken to me throughout my own struggles, how I grew up listening to the sounds of black America and have an everlasting love for a music, as Werner says, that is simply far from my 'own'.[297] Another regret is how the limitations of a word count and time to research has cut this writing short, and how the voices of all those who played a role within the black freedom struggle, through the music industry cannot be extensively recognised. But, as Guralnick states the remembrance of both rhythm and blues and soul is through the work of 'manic record collectors' and 'obsessive DJs… and those who simply fell – by default or fate' for the two styles, all of which I make no failure in identifying with.[298] On the whole, this writing has hoped to express that, as Ellison rightly points out, 'music [and those behind it] rather than politics has provided the real voice of black America' and its history.[299]

---

[297] C. Werner, *A Change is Gonna Come*, p.xvi
[298] M. Guillory & R. C. Green., *Soul: Black Power, Politics, and Pleasure* (London, 1998), p. 116
[299] M. Ellison, *Lyrical Protest*, p.146

About the Author

Annabel May Polles was born in the post-industrial city of Stoke-on-Trent in the late 1990s. Echoes of struggles after the decline of the major pottery industry that was the main feature of Stoke, and the ex-mining community, still preside in the area. However, it was home to a legendary Northern Soul following and the Golden Torch Soul Club, so it was evident that black music would be a huge part of her life growing up and stay with her until adulthood.

Starting an undergraduate degree at Keele University in October of 2017, her passion for studying and history flourished immensely. Furthering those studies in September 2020, Annabel began to study for a Master of Arts degree in History and resurrected a passion for black history that she found during her

A-Level course. Winning the Keele University Postgraduate Conference for her poster submission in 2021, Annabel completed her research, which has become this book, to a high standard. Graduating with a Distinction, she also won the Keele University Margaret Spufford Prize for best history research and thesis in her MA and MRes cohort.

She is currently working within Stoke-on-Trent libraries and continues to spread her passion through book displays and discussions with others.

She has been heavily influenced by the sounds of Black America and Jamaica. The music styles of soul, rhythm & blues, reggae, ska and rocksteady will forever hold a unique and special place in her heart.

Bibliography

Records

1. Booker T & The MG's, *Green Onions* (Reissue, Atlantic, 1979)

2. Booker T & The MG's, *Green Onions* (Stax, 1962)

3. Brown, J. *Say it Loud (I'm Black and I'm Proud)* (King, 1968)

4. Carmichael, S., *Free Huey* (Black Forum, 1970)

5. Chronixx, *Black is Beautiful (Chronology),* (Soul Circle Music/Virgin EMI, 2017)

6. Dave, *Black (Psychodrama),* (Neighbourhood Recordings, 2019)

7. Gaye M. & Weston, K., *It Takes Two* (Tamla, 1966)

8. Gaye, M., *Inner City Blues (Make Me Wanna Holler)* (Tamla, 1971)

9. Hughes L., & Danner, M., *Writers of the Revolution* (Black Forum, 1970)

10. Johnson, S., *Is It Because I'm Black* (Twilight Records, 1970)

11. Jones, W. *Where's My Money* (Peacock, 1963)

12. King, B. E., *Stand By Me* (Atco, 1961)

13. M. L. King, *The Great March to Freedom* (Gordy, 1963)

14. Marley, D & Nas., *Distant Relatives* (Def Jam Recordings, 2010)

15. Pickett, W., *634-5789 (Soulsville, U.S.A),* (Atlantic, 1966)

16. Reeves M. & The Vandellas, *Heatwave* (Gordy, 1963)

17. Reeves M. & The Vandellas, *Nowhere to Run* (1965)

18. Reeves, M. & The Vandellas, *Dancing in the Street* (Gordy, 1964)

19. Springsteen, B. *American Skin (41 Shots),* (Columbia, 2001)

20. Starr, E. *Back Street* (Ric-Tic, 1966)

21. The Temptations, *Ball of Confusion (Gordy, 1970)*

22. The Temptations, *Cloud 9* (Gordy, 1969)

23. The Velvelettes, 'Ain't No Place Like Motown', *A Cellarful Of Motown, Motown* (Album, 2002)

24. The World Column, *So Is The Sun* (Tower, 1969)

25. Walker, Jr & The All-Stars, *Shotgun* (Soul, 1965)

26. Wilson, J., *Beautiful Day* (Brunswick, 1972)

Primary Sources

1. '125,000 Walk Quietly in Record Rights Plea' *Detroit Free Press,* June 24, 1963

2. 'A Night To Remember for Dr. King Fund' *Billboard Magazine*, July 13, 1968

3. 'A Staxed Deck' *Cash Box Magazine*, November 2, 1968

4. 'A Year On Its Own, Stax/Volt Presents A Full Force Image' *Cash Box Magazine*, May 24, 1969

5. 'All Music Firms Part Of U.S.'s 1963 Economic Census' *Cash Box Magazine*, October 19, 1963

6. 'Atlantic-NATRA 'Soul Together' Set for Mad Sq. Garden 6/28' *Cash Box Magazine,* May 18, 1968

7. 'Bios Of Leading Artists Of 1969' *Cash Box Magazine*, December 27, 1969

8. 'Booker T & The MG's: Recording stars have made Memphis soul sound into major musical commodity' *Ebony Magazine*, (1969)

9. 'Carnegie Benefit Bill: Frank Sinatra & Lena Horne' *Cash Box Magazine*, September 21, 1963

10. 'Dooto To Handle Rev. King Disks' *Cash Box Magazine*, August 11, 1962

11. 'Dr. Martin Luther King, Jr. Memorial Albums' *Cash Box Magazine*, May 4, 1968

12. *'Elaine Brown' Album Cover* available in, Sykes, C. E., "The Black Forum Label: Motown Joins the Revolution." *ARSC journal* 46.1 (2015)

13. 'FCC Bans Bias At Broadcast Outlets' *Cash Box Magazine*, July 20, 1968

14. 'Free At Last (Gordy's latest tribute)' *Billboard Magazine*, June 22, 1968

15. *'Free Huey' Album Cover* available in, Sykes, C. E., "The Black Forum Label: Motown Joins the Revolution." *ARSC journal* 46.1 (2015)

16. 'Key Promotions & Additions at Stax/Volt' *Cash Box Magazine*, October 12, 1968

17. 'Labels Answer King Speech Suit' *Cash Box Magazine*, October 19, 1963

18. 'Looking Like A Million Seller...' *Billboard Magazine*, April 17, 1965

19. 'Memphis is what's happening... Thanks to Jim Stewart' *Cash Box Magazine*, February 19, 1966

20. 'Memphis sound: a southern view' *Billboard Magazine*, June 12, 1969

21. 'Motown At NATRA Fete' *Cash Box Magazine*, July 13, 1968

22. 'Motown At Poor People's Rally' *Cash Box Magazine*, May 18, 1968

23. 'Motown, U.S.A., the Convention Way: Record LP Release, Record Billings' *Billboard Magazine,* September 9, 1967

24. 'Music Shops Hit By Ghetto Violence' *Cash Box Magazine*, April 20, 1968

25. 'N.Y. Group Formed To 'Sing' For Civil Rights' *Cash Box Magazine*, October, May 1963

26. 'NATRA, 'New Deejay Responsibilities', Farmer, Others Speak' *Cash Box Magazine*, August 30, 1969

27. 'New & fantastic From Stax-Volt!' *Cash Box Magazine*, November 26, 1966

28. 'Proceeds from the Fest Will Go to Poor People's Campaign' *Billboard Magazine,* August 10, 1968

29. 'Redding, Thomas Lead The Parade In Chicago' *Cash Box Magazine*, August 26, 1969

30. 'Redding's 'Dock' Soars After Tragedy' *The Tennessean Sun,* April 14, 1968

31. 'Seminary Students Work & Sing vs. Anti-Poverty' *Cash Box Magazine*, April 8, 1967

32. 'Set Civil Rights Caravan in Miss. This Summer' *Cash Box Magazine*, June 6, 1964

33. 'Stations Sooth Racial Tensions' *Billboard Magazine*, June 26, 1968

34. 'Stax 1st Single' *Billboard Magazine*, April 17, 1965

35. 'Stax Records Define the Memphis Sound' *The Arizona Republic,* June 24, 1969

36. 'Stax Starts Creative Services Operation' *Cash Box Magazine*, February 22, 1969

37. 'Stax Stay In School LP Part Of Public Service Thing' *Billboard Magazine*, September 9, 1967

38. 'Stax/Volt Augments Promo Force' *Cash Box Magazine*, October 4, 1969

39. 'Stewart: Memphis Soundmaker' *Billboard Magazine*, August 20, 1966

40. 'Tamla-Motown Make Mark in Britain; Gordy, 'Family' Arrive' *Billboard Magazine,* April 3, 1965

41. 'The Billboard The World's Foremost Amusement Weekly' *Billboard Magazine ,* June 25, 1949

42. 'The Death of Dr. Martin Luther King: Trade's Response To Tragedy Is One Of Aid & Comfort' *Cash Box Magazine*, April 20, 1968

43. 'The Memphis Sound… A new music discovered for all people discovered' *Johnson City Press-Chronicle,* March 19, 1969

44. 'The Supremes' *Billboard Magazine*, January 9, 1965

45. 'Tuning In On: KATZ- St. Louis A Black Power House' *Cash Box Magazine*, October 11, 1969

46. 'We're Making HAY While the Sun's Shining…' *Billboard Magazine*, January 23, 1965

47. *Billboard Magazine 1894 – 2017* (Online) Available at: https://worldradiohistory.com/Archive-All-Music/Billboard-Magazine.htm

48. *Black Forum Label Discography* available in, Sykes, C. E., "The Black Forum Label: Motown Joins the Revolution." *ARSC journal* 46.1 (2015)

49. *Cash Box Magazine 1942 – 1996* (Online) Available at: https://worldradiohistory.com/Archive-All-Music/Cash-Box-Magazine.htm

50. *Civil Rights Act 1964*

51. Civil Rights Digital Library, *Series of WSB-TV news film clips of African Americans celebrating and demonstrating as they prepare for the Poor People's March on Washington* (1968) (Online) Available at: http://crdl.usg.edu/cgi/crdl?format=_video;query=id:ugabma_wsbn_wsbn44591

52. Civil Rights Digital Library, *WSB-TV news film clip of students singing freedom songs and Christmas carols in front of the home of Ivan Allen, Junior, mayor of Atlanta, Georgia* (1963) (Online) Available at: http://crdl.usg.edu/cgi/crdl?format=_video;query=id:ugabma_wsbn_wsbn45946

53. Civil Rights Library of St Augustine, *Singing Freedom Songs* (1964) (Online) Available at: https://cdm16000.contentdm.oclc.org/digital/collection/p16000coll3/id/76

54. Civil Rights Library of St Augustine, *Singing Freedom Songs During a March* (1964) (Online) Available at: https://cdm16000.contentdm.oclc.org/digital/collection/p16000coll3/id/87

55. Clark, K. & Baldwin J., in 'The Negro and the American Promise,' *GBH Archives* (46:14 minutes) Available at: https://www.youtube.com/watch?v=TNQGhsPb7U4

56. CRMVet, *The Student Voice and SNCC Internal Newsletters* (1960-1968) (Online) Available at: https://www.crmvet.org/docs/sv/sv.htm

57. Detroit Historical Society, *The Great March to Freedom* (Online) Available at: https://detroithistorical.pastperfectonline.com/archive/E8BD6C

51-A7C8-44B9-A033-254882954020

58. Detroit Historical Society, *The Motown Sound flyer* (1966) (Online) Available at: https://detroithistorical.pastperfectonline.com/archive/68D0A489-8515-4A9C-BCDE-561117777476

59. Detroit Public Library Digital Collections, *Banner* (Online) Available at: https://digitalcollections.detroitpubliclibrary.org/islandora/object/islandora%3A142803

60. Detroit Public Library Digital Collections, *Black and white photographic print of Governor George Romney and Mayor Jerome Cavanaugh at the front of a 10,000 person march in solidarity with the 1965 Selma to Montgomery voting rights marches* (1965) (Online) Available at: https://detroithistorical.pastperfectonline.com/photo/272A6243-6159-47A8-85AD-921838009685

61. Detroit Public Library Digital Collections, *Ford automobiles on assembly line* (Online) Available at: https://digitalcollections.detroitpubliclibrary.org/islandora/object/islandora%3A186522

62. Detroit Public Library Digital Collections, *Motown fan club buttons* (Online) Available at: https://digitalcollections.detroitpubliclibrary.org/islandora/object/islandora%3A163024

63. Detroit Public Library Digital Collections, *Motown Records headquarters, Hitsville U.S.A* (Online) Available at: https://digitalcollections.detroitpubliclibrary.org/islandora/object/islandora%3A163077

64. Detroit Public Library Digital Collections, *Pearl's fashions storefront window painted with 'Soul Sister'* (Online) Available at:

https://digitalcollections.detroitpubliclibrary.org/islandora/object/islandora%3A215601

65. Detroit Public Library Digital Collections, *Storefront window painted with 'Soul brother'* (Online) Available at: https://digitalcollections.detroitpubliclibrary.org/islandora/object/islandora%3A215599

66. Dig Memphis, *Beale Street march* (Online) Available at: https://memphislibrary.contentdm.oclc.org/digital/collection/p13039coll2/id/41/rec/59

67. Dig Memphis, *Civil Rights: Memphis Blues* (Online) Available at: https://memphislibrary.contentdm.oclc.org/digital/collection/p13039coll2/id/633/rec/13

68. Dig Memphis, *Estelle Axton* (Online) Available at: https://memphislibrary.contentdm.oclc.org/digital/collection/p16108coll6/id/205/rec/19

69. Dig Memphis, *I Am a Man Protest* (Online) Available at: https://memphislibrary.contentdm.oclc.org/digital/collection/p13039coll2/id/88/rec/127

70. Dig Memphis, *King Memorial and Funeral Program* (Online) Available at: https://memphislibrary.contentdm.oclc.org/digital/collection/p13039coll2/id/182/rec/136

71. Dig Memphis, *Lorraine Motel Courtyard* (Online) Available at: https://memphislibrary.contentdm.oclc.org/digital/collection/p13039coll2/id/91/rec/191

72. Dig Memphis, *Stax Recording Studios* (Online) Available at: https://memphislibrary.contentdm.oclc.org/digital/collection/p13039coll5/id/3070/rec/13

73. Dig Memphis, *The Future Depends on You the Youth of Memphis* (Online) Available at: https://memphislibrary.contentdm.oclc.org/digital/collection/p13039coll2/id/113/rec/258

74. *Ebony Magazine* (Johnson Publishing Company, 1960, 1961, 1962, 1963, 1964, 1965, 1966, 1967, 1968, 1969) (Online) Available at: https://books.google.co.uk/books?id=PtMDAAAAMBAJ&source=gbs_all_issues_r&cad=1&atm_aiy=1960#all_issues_anchor

75. Ellis, D. A (Motown Museum)., Aerial *Photograph of Freedom March* (1963) Available by request

76. Ellis, D. A (Motown Museum)., *Atlanta Journal 'Songs Give Poor Marchers Life After Day of Waiting'* (1968) Available by request

77. Ellis, D. A (Motown Museum)., *Esther Gordy Edwards, Sr. Vice President of Motown Records, Resurrection City, Washington DC* (1968) Available by request

78. Ellis, D. A (Motown Museum)., *Fuller Gordy of Motown Records Resurrection City, Washington D.C.,* (1968) Available by request

79. Ellis, D. A (Motown Museum)., *Gordy, his wife and Alberta King.* Available by request

80. Ellis, D. A (Motown Museum)., *Image from TERP City of Hope* (2020) Available at:

HTTP://TERP.UMD.EDU/CITY-OF-HOPE/

81. Ellis, D. A (Motown Museum)., *Jet Magazine 'Motown Stars Raise $25,000 For Poor Campaign'* (1968) Available by request

82. Ellis, D. A (Motown Museum)., King and *Gordy holding The Great March to Freedom Album Cover*. Available by request

83. Ellis, D. A (Motown Museum)., Official Programme Front Cover of the Walk to Freedom March (1963) Available by request

84. Face To Face Africa, *Aretha Franklin's touching performance at Martin Luther King's funeral* (1968) (Video) (Online) Available at:https://face2faceafrica.com/article/watch-aretha-franklins-touching-performance-at-martin-luther-kings-funeral

85. Farmer, J., *Freedom When?* (Manhattan, 1966)

86. Indiana University Bloomington, *Booker T. Jones* (Online) Available at: http://webapp1.dlib.indiana.edu/images/item.htm?id=http://purl.dlib.indiana.edu/iudl/images/VAD5464/VAD5464-000061&scope=images/VAD5464

87. Indiana University Bloomington, Carla Thomas (Online) Available at: http://webapp1.dlib.indiana.edu/images/item.htm?id=http://purl.dlib.indiana.edu/iudl/images/VAD5464/VAD5464-000119&scope=images/VAD5464

88. *James Brown promoting a voter registration drive (p.391)* available in, Ward, B., *Just My Soul Responding Rhythm and Blues, Black Consciousness and Race Relations* (London,

1998)

89. *Kerner Commission*, 1967

90. Life, *Martin Luther King Jr. (seated, at right) watched The Shirelles perform during the Salute to Freedom benefit concert in Birmingham* (1963) (Online) Available at:.https://www.life.com/history/march-on-washington-rare-photos-from-a-star-studded-fundraiser-1963/

91. M. L. King, *Great March to Freedom Rally Speech* (1963) Online (Available at: https://www.youtube.com/watch?v=0aO7mXbx2lo)

92. Mann, J., '*Negroes Here Pledge More Demonstrations*' Detroit Free Press (June, 1963)

93. *Martin Luther King Quote at Atlanta for the annual NATRA convention* available in, Ward, B., *Just My Soul Responding Rhythm and Blues, Black Consciousness and Race Relations* (London, 1998)

94. Mid-South Coliseum Collection, *a database of concerts that took place at the Coliseum in Memphis*, (Online) Available at: (https://memphislibrary.contentdm.oclc.org/digital/collection/coliseum/id/62/rec/11)

95. Rise Up North Detroit, *"We Shall Overcome" by Reverend Albert B. Cleage* (1963) (Online) Available at: The National Civil Rights Movement in Detroit - The North | Detroit (riseupdetroit.org)

96. Rise Up North Detroit, *A flyer for the Selective Patronage Campaign asks shoppers to boycott Sears stores with discriminatory hiring practices. "Don't buy where you can't work."* (Online) Available at:

https://riseupdetroit.org/chapters/chapter-3/part-1/the-national-civil-rights-movement-in-detroit/

97. Rise Up North Detroit, *Clip from a 2018 interview with former City Councilwoman JoAnn Watson, in which she discusses Rev. Dr. Martin Luther King, Jr.'s 1963 Walk to Freedom in Detroit* (Online) Available at: https://riseupdetroit.org/chapters/chapter-3/part-1/the-national-civil-rights-movement-in-detroit/

98. Stax Archives, *Children's Books* (Online) Available at: http://staxarchives.com/books-landing.php

99. Stax Archives, *Gettin' It All Together Advertisement* (Online) Available at: http://www.staxarchives.com/gettin-it-all-together-detail.php?id=1

100. Stax Archives, *Guts is music you feel Advertisement* (Online) Available at: http://www.staxarchives.com/ads-detail.php?ad=40

101. Stax Archives, *Roots Advertisement* (Online) Available at: http://www.staxarchives.com/ads-detail.php?ad=41

102. Stax Archives, *Stax Fax* (Online) Available at: http://staxarchives.com/staxfax-landing.php

103. Stax Archives, *Stax Fax Issue 1* (1968), (Online) Available at: http://staxarchives.com/staxfax-book-sf1.php

104. Stax Archives, *Stax Fax Issue 10 (September, 1969)* (Online) Available at: http://staxarchives.com/staxfax-book-sf10.php

105.   Stax Archives, *Stax Fax Issue 11 (1969) (Online) Available at:* http://staxarchives.com/staxfax-book-sf11.php

106.   *Stax Archives, Stax Fax Issue 12 (March, 1970) Available at:* http://staxarchives.com/staxfax-book-sf12.php

107.   Stax Archives, *Stax Fax Issue 2* (1968), (Online) Available at: http://staxarchives.com/staxfax-book-sf2.php

108.   Stax Archives, *Stax Fax Issue 3* (January, 1969), (Online) Available at: http://staxarchives.com/staxfax-book-sf3.php

109.   Stax Archives, *Stax Fax Issue 4* (February, 1969), (Online) Available at: http://staxarchives.com/staxfax-book-sf4.php

110.   Stax Archives, *Stax Fax Issue 5 (March, 1969),* (Online) Available at: http://staxarchives.com/staxfax-book-sf5.php

111.   Stax Archives, *Stax Fax Issue 6 (April, 1969)* (Online) Available at: http://staxarchives.com/staxfax-book-sf6.php

112.   Stax Archives, *Stax Fax Issue 7 (May, 1969)* (Online) Available at: http://staxarchives.com/staxfax-book-sf7.php

113.   Stax Archives, *Stax Fax Issue 8 (June, 1969)* (Online) Available at: http://staxarchives.com/staxfax-book-sf8.php

114.   Stax Archives, *Stax Fax Issue 9 (August, 1969)* (Online) Available at: http://staxarchives.com/staxfax-book-sf10.php

115.   Teach Rock, *Ambassador Andrew Young Discussing the impact of Curtis Mayfield & The Impressions' music on the*

Civil Rights Movement (2007) (Video) (Online) Available at: https://teachrock.org/lesson/music-and-the-movement-giving-voice/

116. Tennessee Virtual Archive, *'Memphis Sound' Grew From Stax* (Online) Available at: https://teva.contentdm.oclc.org/digital/collection/p15138coll18/id/873/rec/3

117. Tennessee Virtual Archive, *Stax Backers' Talk Sounds Like Broken Record* (Online) Available at: https://teva.contentdm.oclc.org/digital/collection/p15138coll18/id/900/rec/1

118. Tennessee Virtual Archive, *Stax Records The Dream That Died* (Online) Available at: https://teva.contentdm.oclc.org/digital/collection/p15138coll18/id/874/rec/3

119. University of Mississippi Libraries, *Citizens' Council Collection* (Online) Available at: https://libraries.olemiss.edu/cedar-archives/finding_aids/MUM00072.html

120. University of Newcastle Upon Tyne Oral History Collection, *Shelley Stewart interview with Brian Ward (*29/10/1995)

121. *Voting Rights Act 1965*

122. Washington State University, *Nancy Nelson sings two civil rights spirituals* (2001) (Online) Available at: https://content.libraries.wsu.edu/digital/collection/cvoralhist/id/14

123. Wayne State University Libraries, *Gordy, Berry Jr.; President Motown Records* (Online) Available at: https://digital.library.wayne.edu/item/wayne:vmc26608

124. Wayne State University Libraries, *Gordy, Berry Jr.; President Motown Records (Small Business Week)* (Online) Available at: https://digital.library.wayne.edu/item/wayne:vmc26608_1

125. Wayne State University Libraries, *King, Martin Luther; Negro Leader – Freedom Parade* (1963) (Online) Available at: https://digital.library.wayne.edu/item/wayne:vmc53524_2

126. Wayne State University Libraries, *Lansing Demonstration* (1960) (Online) Available at: https://digital.library.wayne.edu/item/wayne:vmc1125

127. Wayne State University Libraries, Motown Record Corporation; Exterior of Hitsville, U.S.A (Online) Available at: https://digital.library.wayne.edu/item/wayne:vmc52439

128. Wayne State University Libraries, *Music Hall Theatre. Detroit,* (Online) Available at: https://digital.library.wayne.edu/item/wayne:vmc66518_1

129. Wayne State University Libraries, *Robinson, Smokey; Singer-Composer* Smokey Robinson performs to an enthusiastic crowd in Downtown Detroit (1969) (Online) Available at: https://digital.library.wayne.edu/item/wayne:vmc65278_3

130. Wayne State University Walter P. Reuther Library, *NAACP Detroit Branch Reocrds* (Online) Available at: https://reuther.wayne.edu/files/UR000244_0.pdf

131. Wayne State Unviersity Libraries, *The Detroit Sunday Journal Motown magic* (1998) (Online) Available at: https://digital.library.wayne.edu/item/wayne:DSJv3i14DSJ19980215

Secondary

1. Albert, P. J., & Hoffman, R., *We Shall Overcome: Martin Luther King, Jr., and the Black Freedom Struggle* (New York, 1993)

2. Badger, A. J., *New Deal / New South* (Fayetteville, 2007)

3. Ballantyne, D. T., *New Politics in the Old South: Ernest F Hollings in the Civil Rights Era* (South Carolina, 2016)

4. Ballantyne, D., 'A Public Problem Rather Than a Question of Social Welfare: Ernest F. Hollings and the Politics of Hunger' in, *The Sixties* 8.1 (2015)

5. Ballantyne, K., 'We Might Overcome Someday: West Tennessee's Rural Freedom Movement', *Journal of Contemporary History 56.1* (2021)

6. Balu, R., & Wood, S., 'Politics, Race and a Little Rhythm & Blues: Profile of Civil Rights Activist Jerry Butler', *Human Rights 23.1* (1996)

7. Baraka, A., *Blues People: Negro Music in White America* (1980)

8. Batho, N., 'Black Power Children's Literature: Julius Lester and Black Power', *Journal of American Studies*

(2019),

9. BBC, *Roe v Wade: What is the US Supreme Court Ruling on Abortion?* (2020) (Online) Available at: https://www.bbc.co.uk/news/world-us-canada-54513499

10. Beifuss, J. T., *At the River I Stand: Memphis, the 1968 Strike and Martin Luther King* (New York, 1989)

11. Biggs, A., 'Protest Campaigns and Movement Success: Desegregating the U.S. South in the Early 1960s', *American Sociological Review 80.2* (2015)

12. Black History Month, *Marcus Garvey Famously Wrote* (2020) (Online) Available at: https://www.blackhistorymonth.org.uk/article/section/bhm-intros/marcus-garvey-famously-wrote-a-people%E2%80%AFwithout%E2%80%AFknowledge-of-their-past-history-origin-and-culture-is-like-a%E2%80%AFtree-without-roots/

13. Black History Month, *Motown at 60… A Legacy To Be Remembered* (2020) (Online) Available at: https://www.blackhistorymonth.org.uk/article/section/music-entertainers/motown-at-60-a-legacy-to-be-remembered/

14. Bowman, R., *Soulsville, USA: The story of Stax Records* (New York, 1997)

15. Boyce, A.K., *"What's Going On": Motown and the Civil Rights Movement* (Boston, Massachusetts, 2008)

16. Branch, T., *The King Years: Historic Moments in the Civil Rights Movement* (New York, 2013)

17. Brattain, M., 'Miscegenation and Competing Definitions of Race in Twentieth-Century Louisiana', *Journal of Southern History 71.3* (2005)

18. Bretz, B., 'The Poor People's Campaign: An Evolution of the Civil Rights Movement', *Sociological Viewpoints* (2010)

19. Brewer, J., 'Microhistory and the Histories of Everyday Life', *Cultural and social history* 7:1 (2015)

20. Brewer, R., 'String Musicians in the Recording Studios of Memphis, Tennessee', *Popular Music* 19.2 (2000)

21. Brown, L., 'Remembering Silence: Bennett College Women and the 1960 Greensboro Student Sit-Ins', *Rhetoric Society Quarterly* 48:1 (2018)

22. Burke, P., *History and Social Theory* (1992)

23. Carawan, G., & Carawan, C., *Freedom Is a Constant Struggle: Songs of the Freedom Movement* (New York, 1968)

24. Cha-Jua, S. K., & Lang, C., 'The 'Long Movement' as Vampire: Temporal and Spatial Fallacies in Recent Black Freedom Studies', *Journal of African American History 92.2* (2007)

25. Chow, A.R., *How Martin Luther King Jr. and Motown Saved the Sound of the Civil Rights Movement* (2020)

(Online) Available at: https://time.com/5783939/mlk-jr-dream-speech-motown/

26. Chuck, E., 'Southern Soul: A User's Guide', *The Village Voice* 56.10 (New York, 2011)

27. Cobb, J. C., 'Somebody Done Nailed Us on the Cross: Federal Farm and Welfare Policy and the Civil Rights Movement in the Mississippi Delta', *Journal of American History* 77.3 (Indiana, 1990)

28. Cone, J. H., 'Martin and Malcolm and America: A dream or a nightmare?' in *Martin Luther King, Jr and the Civil Rights Movement,* ed J. A. Kirk (Hampshire, 2007)

29. Cosgrove, S. *Memphis '68: The Tragedy of Southern Soul* (Edinburgh, 2018)

30. Cosgrove, S., *Detroit '67 The Year That Changed Soul* (Edinburgh, 2016)

31. Coulangeon, P., et al., 'Music and social movements: Mobilizing Traditions in the Twentieth Century', *Revue Française de Sociologie* 40.1 (1999)

32. Crosby, E., ''It Wasn't the Wild West' Keeping Local Studies in Self Defence Historiography' in *Civil Rights History from the Ground Up Local Struggles, A National Movement,* ed. E. Crosby (Georgia, Atlanta, 2011) 194-255

33. Crosby, E., 'White Privilege, Black Burden: Lost Opportunities and Deceptive Narratives in School Desegregation in Claiborne County, Mississippi', *Oral*

History Review (2012)

34. Crosby, E., *Civil Rights Struggles from the Ground Up: Local Struggles, a National Movement* (Georgia, Atlanta, 2011)

35. Danielson, J., *The Role of Soul: Stax Records and the Civil Rights Movement in Memphis, Tennessee,* (ProQuest Dissertations Publishing, 2015) Available at: https://lib.dr.iastate.edu/cgi/viewcontent.cgi?article=5694&context=etd

36. Davies, T., 'Black Power in Action: The Bedford-Stuyvesant Restoration Corporation, Robert F. Kennedy, and the Politics of the Urban Crisis', *Journal of American History 100.3* (2013)

37. De Jong, G., 'Staying in Place: Black Migration, the Civil Rights Movement, and the War on Poverty in the Rural South', *Journal of African American History 90.4* (2005)

38. De Jong, G., *You Can't Eat Freedom: Southerners and Social Justice after the Civil Rights Movement* (Chapel Hill, North Carolina, 2016)

39. Dierenfield, B. J., *The Civil Rights Movement* (2013)

40. Dinerstein, J., 'The Soul Roots of Bruce Springsteen's American Dream', *Journal of Popular Culture 17.2* (1983)

41. Duke University Libraries, *Julian Bond* (Online) Available at: https://snccdigital.org/people/julian-bond/

42. Duke University, *The Civil Rights Movement: Grass Roots Perspectives* (Online) Available at:

https://sites.duke.edu/dukecrmsummerinstitute/summer-institute/

43. Dwyer, O. J., 'Interpreting the Civil Rights Movement Contradiction, Confirmation, and the Cultural Landscape, in *The Civil Rights Movement in American Memory* ed. C. R. Romano & L. Raiford (Georgia, 1992)

44. Dybska, A., 'Where the War on Poverty and Black Power Meet: A Right to the City Perspective on American Urban Politics in the 1960s', *European Journal of American Studies 10.3* (2015)

45. <u>E. B. Freedman, *Redefining Rape: Sexual Violence in the Era of Suffrage and Segregation* (Massachusetts, 2013)</u>

46. Ellis, D. A (Motown Museum)., *TERP City of Hope* (2020) Available at: HTTP://TERP.UMD.EDU/CITY-OF-HOPE/

47. Ellison, M., *Lyrical Protest: Black Music's Struggle Against Discrimination* (New York, 1989)

48. Fairclough, A., 'The Costs of Brown: Black Teachers and School Integration', *Journal of American History* 91.1 (2004)

49. Fairclough, A., *A Study of the Southern Christian Leadership Conference and the Rise and Fall of Nonviolent Civil Rights Movement* (1977)

50. Fairclough, A., *Better Day Coming: Blacks and Equality, 1890-2000* (London, 2002)

51. Fairclough, A., *To Redeem the Soul of America: The Southern Christian Leadership Conference and Martin Luther King, Jr.* (Georgia, 1987)

52. Farmer, J., *Lay Bare the Heart: An Autobiography of the Civil Rights Movement* (Maryland, 1985)

53. Fearnley, A. M., 'The Black Panther Party's Publishing Strategies and the Financial Underpinnings of Activism, 1968 – 1975', *Historical Journal 62.1* (2019)

54. Fine, S., *Expanding the Frontiers of Civil Rights Michigan, 1948- 1968* (Maryland, 2018)

55. Fritsch, J., *The Diallo Verdict: The Overview; 4 Officers In Diallo Shooting Are Acquitted Of All Charges(2000) (Online) Available at:* https://www.nytimes.com/2000/02/26/nyregion/diallo-verdict-overview-4-officers-diallo-shooting-are-acquitted-all-charges.html

56. Garrow, D. J., *The Walking City: The Montgomery Bus Boycott, 1955-1956* (New York, 1989)

57. Garrow, D. J., *We Shall Overcome: The Civil Rights Movement in the United States in the 1950's and 1960's* (New York,1989)

58. George, N, *Where Did Our Love Go?: the Rise & Fall of the Motown Sound* (London, 2003)

59. George, N., *The Death of Rhythm and Blues* (London, 1989)

60. Germany, K. B., 'Poverty Wars in the Louisiana Delta: White Resistance, Black Power, and the Poorest Place in America' in, eds. Orleck, A., & Hazirjian, L. G., *The War On Poverty: A New Grassroots History, 1964-1980* (Athens, 2011)

61. Giovanni, L., 'On Microhistory,' in P. Burke, ed., *New Perspectives on Historical Writing* 2 (2001)

62. Gordon, R., *It Came from Memphis* (Tennessee, 2017)

63. Gordon. R., *Respect Yourself: Stax records and the Soul Explosion* (New York, 2013)

64. Gordy, B., *To Be Loved: the Music, the Magic, the Memories of Motown* (2013)

65. Grant, N., 'Crossing the Black Atlantic: The Global Antiapartheid Movement and the Racial Politics of the Cold War', *Radical History Review 119* (2014)

66. Green, L. B., 'Saving Babies in Memphis: The Politics of Race, Health and Hunger during the War on Poverty' in, eds. Orleck, A., & Hazirjian, L. G., *The War On Poverty: A New Grassroots History, 1964-1980* (Athens, 2011)

67. Green, L., 'Race, Gender, and Labour in 1960s Memphis: 'I Am a Man' and the Meaning of Freedom', *Journal of Urban History 30.3* (2004)

68. Greene, C. 'Someday… the Coloured and White Will Stand Together' The War on Poverty, Black Power Politics, and Southern Women's Interracial Alliances' in, eds. Orleck, A., & Hazirjian, L. G., *The War On Poverty: A New*

Grassroots History, 1964-1980 (Athens, 2011)

69. Gregory, B.S., 'Is Small Beautiful? Micro-history and the History of Everyday Life,' *History and Theory*, 38:1 (1999)

70. Gritter, E., 'Black Memphians and New Frontiers: The Shelby County Democratic Club, the Kennedy Administration, and the Quest for Black Political Power, 1959-64' in, eds. Goudsouzian, A & McKinney Jr, C. W., *An Unseen Light: Black Struggles for Freedom in Memphis, Tennessee* (Kentucky, 2018)

71. Guillory, M., & Green, R. C., *Soul: Black Power, Politics, and Pleasure* (New York, 1997)

72. Guralnick, P., *Sweet Soul Music: Rhythm and Blues and the Southern Dream of Freedom* (Edinburgh, 2002)

73. Haider, A., *Motown: The music that changed America* (2019) (Online) Available at: https://www.bbc.com/culture/article/20190109-motown-the-music-that-changed-america

74. Hall, S., 'On the Tail of the Panther: Black Power and the 1967 Convention of the National Conference for New Politics', *Journal of American Studies* (2003)

75. Hall, S., 'The NAACP, Black Power, and the African American Freedom Struggle, 1966-1969', *The Historian* (2007)

76. Hall, S., 'The Response of the Moderate Wing of the Civil Rights Movement to the War in Vietnam', *Historical*

Journal (2003)

77. Haralambos, M., *Right On: From Blues to Soul in Black America* (London, 1974)

78. Hill, L., 'The Deacons for Defence: Armed Resistance and the Civil Rights Movement' in *Martin Luther King, Jr and the Civil Rights Movement,* ed J. A. Kirk (Hampshire, 2007) 86-94

79. Hughes, C. L., '"You pay one hell of a price to be black': Rufus Thomas and the Racial Politics of Memphis Music' in, eds. Goudsouzian, A & McKinney Jr, C. W., *An Unseen Light: Black Struggles for Freedom in Memphis, Tennessee* (Kentucky, 2018)

80. Hughes, C. L., *Country Soul: Making Music and Making Race in the American South* (Chapel Hill, North Carolina, 2015)

81. Jackson, P. S. B., 'The Crisis of the 'Disadvantaged Child': Poverty Research, IQ, and Muppet Diplomacy in the 1960s' in, *Antipode 46.1* (2014)

82. Jones, B. T., *Time is Tight: My Life, Note by Note* (New York, 2017)

83. Jones, L., *Black Music* (New York, 1980)

84. Joseph, P. E., 'The Black Power Movement: A State of the Field', *Journal of American History 96.3* (2009)

85. Justman, P. et al., *Standing in the Shadows of Motown*, Momentum Pictures, 2003. Film

86. Kernodle, T. L., '"I Wish I Knew How it Would Feel to Be Free": Nina Simone and the Redefining of the Freedom Song of the 1960s', *Journal of the Society for American Music 2.3* (2008)

87. Kinchen, S. J., 'Black Power in the Bluff City: African American Youth and Student Activism in Memphis, 1965-1975', *Journal of Pan African Studies* (2016)

88. King, M. E., *Freedom Song a Personal Story of the 1960s Civil Rights Movement* (New York, 1987)

89. Kirk, J. A., 'State of the Art: Martin Luther King, Jr.', *Journal of American Studies* (2004)

90. Kirk, J. A., *Martin Luther King Jr.* (Harlow, 2005)

91. Kirk, J. A., *Martin Luther King, Jr. and the Civil Rights Movement: Controversies and Debates* (Basingstoke, 2007)

92. Kofsky, F., *Black Nationalism and the Revolution in Music* (New York, 1973)

93. Kornbluh, F., 'Black Buying Power: Welfare Rights, Consumerism, and Northern Protest', in eds. Theoharis, J. & Woodward, K., *Freedom North: Black Freedom Struggles Outside the South, 1940-1980* (New York, 2003)

94. Kornbluh, F., 'Food as a Civil Right: Hunger, Work and Welfare in the South after the Civil Rights Act' in, *Labour 12.1-2* (North Carolina, 2015)

95. Kornbluh, F., *The Battle for Welfare Rights: Politics and Poverty in Modern America* (Philadelphia, 2007)

96. Korstad, R., & Lichtenstein, N., 'Opportunities Found and Lost: Labour, Radicals, and the Early Civil Rights Movement', *Journal of American History 75.3* (1988)

97. Kowal, R., 'Staging the Greensboro Sit-ins' *Drama Review* 48:4 (2004)

98. Lang, C., 'Locating the Civil Rights Movement: An Essay on the Deep South, Midwest, and Border South in Black Freedom Studies', *Journal of Social History 47.2* (2013)

99. Lassiter, M.D., 'The Suburban Origins of 'Colour-Blind' Conservatism', *Journal of Urban History 30.4* (2004)

100. Laurent, S., 'Is Violence Sometimes a Legitimate Right? An African-American Dilemma', *Diogenes 61.3-4* (2014)

101. Lewis, J. & D'Orso M., *Walking With the Wind* (1998)

102. Lisle, A., *Soulsville: How It All Began* (2019) Online (Available at: https://memphismagazine.com/features/soulsville-how-it-all-began/ (Accessed: 4/5/21)

103. Little, K. K., *You Must Be from the North: Southern White Women in The Memphis Civil Rights Movement* (Jackson, 2009)

104. Litwack, L. F., ''Fight the Power!' The Legacy of the Civil Rights Movement', *Journal of Southern History, 75:*

1 (2009)

105. Mantler, G., 'The Press Did You In: The Poor People's Campaign and the Mass Media', *The Sixties 3.1* (2010)

106. Marsh, D., *The Heart of Rock and Soul: the 1001 Greatest Singles Ever Made* (New York, 2017)

107. Matlin, D. '"Lift Up Yr Self!' Reinterpreting Amiri Baraka (LeRoi Jones), Black Power, and the Uplift Tradition', *Journal of American History 93.1* (2006)

108. Matthews, T. A., '"No One Ever Asks What a Man's Role in the Revolution Is": Gender Politics and Leadership in the Black Panther Party, 1966–71', *Sisters in the Struggle* (2001)

109. Maultsby, P., 'Soul Music: Its Sociological and Political Significance in American Popular Culture', *Journal of Popular Culture 17.2* (1983)

110. McCann, I., *Motown and Martin Luther King Jr.'s I Have A Dream Speech* (2021) (Online) Available at: https://www.udiscovermusic.com/stories/motown-martin-luther-king-i-have-a-dream-speech/

111. McElroy, K., 'You Must Remember This: Obituaries and the Civil Rights Movement', *Journal of Black Studies* 44.4 (2013)

112. McNeil, A., 'The Social Foundations of the Music of Black Americans', *Music Educators Journal 60.6* (1974)

113. Memphis Music Hall of Fame, *Jim Stewart, Estelle Axton* (Online) Available at:

https://memphismusichalloffame.com/inductee/jimstewartestelleaxton/

114. Memphis Music Hall of Fame, *Robert Gordon* (Online) Available at: https://memphismusichalloffame.com/story_author/robert-gordon/

115. Minchin, T. J. & Salmond, J. A., *After the Dream: Black and White Southerners Since 1965* (Lexington, Kentucky, 2011)

116. Minchin, T. J., 'Making Best Use of the New Laws: The NAACP and the Fight for Civil Rights in the South, 1965-1975', *Journal of Southern History 74:3* (2008)

117. Morgan, E. P., 'The Good, the Bad, and the Forgotten Media Culture and Public Memory of the Civil Rights Movement, in *The Civil Rights Movement in American Memory* ed. C. R. Romano & L. Raiford (Georgia, 1992)

118. Motown Museum, *The Sound That Changed America* (Online) Available at: https://www.motownmuseum.org/story/motown/

119. Moye, J. T. 'Focusing Our Eyes on the Prize How community Studies Are Reframing and Rewriting the History of the Civil Rights Movement', in *Civil Rights History from the Ground Up: Local Struggles, a National Movement* eds., E. Crosby (Georgia, 2011)

120. Musgrove, G. D., & Jeffries, H. K., 'The Community Don't Know What's Good for Them: Local Politics in the Alabama Black Belt During the Post–Civil Rights Era',

Freedom Rights (2011)

121. Nasstrom, K. L., 'Between Memory and History: Autobiographies of the Civil Rights Movement and the Writing of Civil Rights History', *Journal of Southern History 74.2* (2008)

122. Newstex Guest Voice, *Aretha Franklin: Sublime Soul Diva Whose Voice Inspired the Civil Rights Movement* (2018)

123. Nnoka, M., 'Race Music, and Interview with Berry Gordy', *The Massachusetts Review 57.4* (2016)

124. Norman, B., 'The Posthumous Autobiography and Civil Rights Memory', *African American Review 53.1* (2020)

125. NPR, *'I Have A Dream' Speech, In Its Entirety* (2010) (Online) Available at: https://www.npr.org/2010/01/18/122701268/i-have-a-dream-speech-in-its-entirety

126. Ogbar, J. O. G., *Black Power Radical Politics and African American Identity* (Maryland, 2004)

127. Patterson, J. T., *America's Struggle Against Poverty, 1900-1994* (Cambridge, 1995)

128. Pavlic, E., & Neal, M. A., 'What the Music Said: Black Popular Music and Black Public Culture' (2000)

129. Perry, I., 'Shall we Overcome?: Music and the Movement', in *May We Forever Stand: A History of the*

Black National Anthem (Chapel Hill, North Carolina, 2018)

130. Potorti, M., 'Feeding the Revolution: The Black Panther Party, Hunger and Community Survival', *Journal of African American Studies* (New Jersey, 2017)

131. ProQuest, *Civil Rights and Black Power Movements (1946 -1975)* (Online) Available at: https://blackfreedom.proquest.com/category/civil-rights-and-black-power-movements/

132. Rachal, J. R., 'We'll Never Turn Back: Adult Education and the Struggle for Citizenship in Mississippi's Freedom Summer', *American Educational Research Journal 35.2* (1998)

133. Rainwater, L., *Behind Ghetto Walls: Black Families in a Federal Slum* (London, 1971)

134. Ransby, B., *Book World: Life for Detroit's Blacks in the 1960s: Vibrant and Volatile* (2017)

135. Reagon, B. J., 'Let the Church Sing Freedom', *Black Music Research Journal 7* (1987)

136. Redmond, S. L., 'Citizens of Sound: Negotiations of Race and Diaspora in the Anthems of the UNIA and NAACP', *African and Black Diaspora: An International Journal 4.1* (2011)

137. Reeves, M. & Bego, M., *Dancing in the Street: Confessions of a Motown Diva* (New York, 1994)

138. Rivers, B., *Flagler Professor's 'From Civil Rights to Black Power in Rock' Lecture to Air on C-SPAN* (2020) (Online) Available at: https://news.wjct.org/post/flagler-professors-civil-rights-black-power-rock-lecture-air-c-span

139. Roach, H., *Black American Music: Past and Present* (Florida, 1992)

140. Roberts, G., and Klibanoff, H., *The Race Beat: The Press, the Civil Rights Struggle, and the Awakening of a Nation* (New York, 2007)

141. Robinson J. A. G. & Garrow, D. J., *The Montgomery Bus Boycott and the Women Who Started It: The Memoir of Jo Ann Gibson Robinson* (Knoxville, 1987)

142. Robinson, S., *Smokey: Inside My Life* (London, 2017)

143. Robinson, Z. F., 'After Stax: Race, Sound and Neighbourhood Revitalisation', in, eds. Goudsouzian, A & McKinney Jr, C. W., *An Unseen Light: Black Struggles for Freedom in Memphis, Tennessee* (Kentucky, 2018)

144. Rose, L. P., 'The Freedom Singers of the Civil Rights Movement: Music Functioning for Freedom', *Applications of Research in Music Education 25.2* (2007)

145. Russell, C., 'A Beautician Without Teacher Training: Bernice Robinson, Citizenship Schools and Women in the Civil Rights Movement', *The Sixties 4.1* (2011)

146. Sampson, T., *Say Happy 90th Birthday to Stax Records Founder Jim Stewart* (2020)

147. Sanders, C. R., 'More than Cookies and Crayons: Head Start and African American Empowerment in Mississippi, 1965-1968', *Journal of African American History 100:4* (2015)

148. Sanders, C. R., 'More than Cookies and Crayons: Head Start and African American Empowerment in Mississippi, 1965-1968', *Journal of African American History 100:4* (2015)

149. Santoro, W., "The Civil Rights Movement and the Right to Vote: Black Protest, Segregationist Violence and the Audience." in, *Social Forces* 86.4 (2008)

150. Schulte, W., & Frederick, N., 'Black Panther and Black Agency: Constructing Cultural Nationalism in Comic Books Featuring Black Panther, 1973-1979', *Journal of Graphic Novels & Comics* 11.3 (2020)

151. Seeger, P. et al., *Everybody Says Freedom* (New York, 1989)

152. Self, R., 'To Plan our Liberation: Black Power and the Politics of Place in Oakland, California, 1965-1977', *Journal of Urban History* 26.6 (2000)

153. Sexton, P., 'Nowhere to Run: Motown Music Casts an Intercontinental Shadow', *Billboard 106.45* (1994)

154. Shaw, A., *Honkers and Shouters: The Golden Years of Rhythm and Blues* (New York, 1978)

155. Shaw, A., *Black Popular Music in America: from the Spirituals, Minstrels, and Ragtime to Soul, Disco, and Hip-*

Hop (New York, 1986)

156. Siracusa, A. C., 'Nonviolence, Black Power and the Surveillance State in Memphis' War on Poverty' in, eds. Goudsouzian, A & McKinney Jr, C. W., *An Unseen Light: Black Struggles for Freedom in Memphis, Tennessee* (Kentucky, 2018)

157. Slobin, M., 'Improvising a Musical Metropolis: Detroit in the 1940s- 1960s', *Ethnomusicology 60.1* (2016)

158. Smart City Memphis, *The Invaders: A Uniquely Memphis Story* (2016) (Online) Available at: https://www.smartcitymemphis.com/2016/11/the-invaders-a-uniquely-memphis-story/

159. Smith, B. J., 'Food and the Mississippi Civil Rights Movement: Re-Reading the 1962-1963 Greenwood Food Blockade.' in, *Food, Culture & Society* 23.3 (2020)
160. Smith, B. J., 'Food and the Mississippi Civil Rights Movement: Re-Reading the 1962-1963 Greenwood Food Blockade.' in, *Food, Culture & Society* 23.3 (2020)

161. Smith, S. E., *Dancing in the Street: Motown and the Cultural Politics of Detroit* (Massachusetts, 1999)

162. Spencer, R. C. & Hogan, W., 'Telling Freedom Stories from the Inside Out: Internal Politics and Movement Cultures in SNCC and the Black Panther Party' in *Civil Rights History from the Ground Up Local Struggles, A National Movement,* ed. E. Crosby (Georgia, 2011) 330-365

163. Springsteen, B., *Born to Run* (New York, 2016)

164. Stax, *Stax Museum of American Soul Music* (Online) Available at: https://staxmuseum.com/

165. Sugrue, T. J., *Sweet Land of Liberty: The Forgotten Struggle for Civil Rights in the North* (New York, 2009)

166. Sugrue, T.J., 'Affirmative Action from Below: Civil Rights, the Building Trades, and the Politics of Racial Equality in the Urban North, 1945–1969', *Journal of American History 91.1* (2004)

167. Sykes, C. E., 'The Black Forum Label: Motown Joins the Revolution', *ARSC Journal 46.1* (2015)

168. Teach Rock, *Andrew Young* (Online) Available at: https://3o9d0y1wloj7e90sc37nviar-wpengine.netdna-ssl.com/wp-content/uploads/L029H01.pdf

169. Tennessee State Government, *Miscegenation* (Online) Available at: https://sharetngov.tnsosfiles.com/tsla/exhibits/blackhistory/pdfs/Miscegenation%20laws.pdf

170. The Gilder Lehrman Institute of American History, *'People Get Ready': Music and the Civil Rights Movement of the 1950s and 1960s* (Online) Available at: https://ap.gilderlehrman.org/history-by-era/civil-rights-movement/essays/%E2%80%9Cpeople-get-ready%E2%80%9D-music-and-civil-rights-movement-1950s

171. The Henry Ford, *Motown's Contribution to the Civil Rights Movement* (2018) (Online) Available at:

https://www.thehenryford.org/explore/blog/motown-s-contribution-to-the-civil-rights-movement

172. Thelen, D., 'Memory and American History', *Journal of American History* 75:4 (Indiana, 1989)

173. Theoharis, J., & Woodard, K., *Freedom North: Black Freedom Struggles Outside the South, 1940-1980* (New York, 2003)

174. Thurber, T., 'February One: The Story of the Greensboro Four' *Magazine History* 20:1 (2006)

175. Tuck, S., *We Ain't What We Ought To Be: The Black Freedom Struggle From Emancipation to Obama* (Massachusetts, 2010)

176. Tuskegee University, *Dr. Booker Taliaferro Washington* (2021) (Online) Available at: https://www.tuskegee.edu/discover-tu/tu-presidents/booker-t-washington

177. Umoja, A. O., *We Will Shoot Back: Armed Resistance in the Mississippi Freedom Movement* (New York, 2013)

178. University Wire, *Connecting Civil Rights with Music* (2019)

179. Waller, D., *The Motown Story* (New York, 1985)

180. Walmsley, M., 'Tell It Like It Isn't: SNCC and the Media, 1960-1965', *Journal of American Studies* 48:1 (2014)

181. Ward, B., and Badger, A. J., *The Making of Martin Luther King and the Civil Rights Movement* (New York, 1996)

182. Ward, B., *Just My Soul Responding: Rhythm and Blues, Black Consciousness and Race Relations* (London, 1998)

183. Ward, J. M., *Hanging Bridge Racial Violence and America's Civil Rights Century* (Oxford, 2016)

184. Webb, C., *Massive Resistance: Southern Opposition to the Second Reconstruction* (New York, 2005)

185. Wendt, S., ''They Finally Found Out That We Are Men': Violence, Non-Violence and Black Manhood in the Civil Rights Era' *Gender & History 19:3* 543-564

186. Wendt, S., "Protection or Path Toward Revolution?: Black Power and Self-Defense." *Souls* (Colorado, 2007)

187. Wendt, S., *The Spirit and the Shotgun Armed Resistance and the Struggle for Civil Rights* (Florida, 2010)

188. Werner, C., *A Change is Gonna Come: Music, Race and the Soul of America* (London, 1998)

189. Werner, C., *Higher Ground: Stevie Wonder, Aretha Franklin, Curtis Mayfield, and the Rise and Fall of American Soul* (New York, 2004)

190. Whitall, S. *Women of Motown: An Oral History* (Tennessee, 2017)

191. Whitlinger, C., & Fretwell, J., 'Political Assassination and Social Movement Outcomes: Martin Luther King and the Memphis Sanitation Workers' Strike', *Sociological Perspectives 62.4* (2019)

192. Williams, J., *Eyes on the Prize: America's Civil Rights Years, 1954-1965 25th Anniversary ed.* (New York, 2013)

193. Williams, O. & Bashe, P. R., *Temptations* (New York, 2017)

194. Wilson, A., *Northern Soul: Music, Drugs and Subcultural Identity* (Cullompton, 2007)

195. Wilson, M., *Dreamgirl and Supreme Faith: My Life as a Supreme* (New York, 1999)

196. WNYC, *Deconstructing Martin Luther King Jr's Dream* (2013) (Online) Available at: https://www.wnyc.org/story/301027-deconstructing-martin-luther-king-jrs-dream/

197. Woodford, W., *All Our Yesterdays: A Brief History of Detroit* (2017)

198. Wright, A. N., 'The 1968 Poor People's Campaign, Marks, Mississippi, and the Mule Train: Fighting Poverty Locally, Representing Poverty Nationally' in E. Crosby, *Civil Rights History From The Ground Up: Local Struggles, A National Movement'* (Georgia, 2011)

199. Wright, G., 'The Civil Rights Revolution as Economic History', *Journal of Economic History 59.2* (1999)

200. Young, A., *An Easy Burden: The Civil Rights Movement and the Transformation of America* (New York, 1996)

Milton Keynes UK
Ingram Content Group UK Ltd.
UKHW010801080923
428296UK00001B/132